Living with a
Yorkshire Terrier

Edited by Richard Haynes

BARRON'S

THE QUESTION OF GENDER
The "he" pronoun is used throughout this book in favor of the rather impersonal "it," but no gender bias is intended at all.

ACKNOWLEDGMENTS
The publisher would like to thank the following for help with photography: Pat Ellington (Patajohn), Wendy White (Wenwytes), and Christine Crowther (Candytops).

First edition for the United States, its territories and dependencies, and Canada published in 2003 by Barron's Educational Series, Inc.

First published in 2003 by Interpet Publishing.

All inquiries should be addressed to:
Barron's Educational Series, Inc.
250 Wireless Boulevard
Hauppauge, New York 11788
http://www.barronseduc.com

International Standard Book Number: 0-7641-5670-5

Library of Congress Catalog Card Number: 2002117160

Printed in Singapore
9 8 7 6 5 4 3 2 1

CONTENTS

CHAPTER ONE

INTRODUCING THE YORKSHIRE TERRIER

Bright, alert, fearless, and feisty – the Yorkshire Terrier is the ultimate big dog in a small package. He is one of the smallest members of the Toy Group, and yet he is a complete scene stealer. The moment a Yorkshire Terrier steps out across a show ring, with his gleaming coat in full flow, there are eyes for no one else.

At home, the Yorkshire Terrier is equally quick to make his presence felt. He takes responsibility for guarding the house, and checking out every new sight and sound he comes across. He is busy and active – and seemingly tireless. This is not a lap dog that is content to spend his day lounging on the sofa; the Yorkie wants to be out and about, and taking charge of the world.

There is another, most endearing side to the Yorkshire Terrier's character. This is a loving, loyal, and affectionate dog that will give his family unique companionship. In many cases, a Yorkie will decide that one member of the family will be special, and this lucky person will be given a wonderful gift of friendship and loyalty.

Clearly, this is a breed with no equal, and anyone who takes on a Yorkie will be content with no other breed.

YORKIE ORIGINS

The history of many dog breeds is lost in the mists of time, and is open to a mixture of folklore and speculation. However, this is not the case with the Yorkshire Terrier. This is a manmade breed, with a relatively recent history, and so we can chart the breed's progress and development with complete accuracy.

To trace the origins of the Yorkie, we need to go back to the Industrial Revolution, which changed the face of Britain from the late 18th century on. As the nation became industrialized, workers were needed in the mills, mines, and factories that were springing up in the new urban centers. Yorkshire soon became a center for industry, and families from Scotland, who were failing to make a living from the land, went south to find work. The families brought as many possessions with them as they could manage, including the family dogs. These were small, native terriers, and would have included the Skye Terrier, which is still around today, plus the Paisley Terrier and the Brokenhaired Scotch Terrier.

At that time, the Skye Terrier was a large dog, weighing around 18 pounds (8.3 kg), with a relatively long, harsh coat, which would have

The Yorkshire Terrier has links with the Skye Terrier and the Maltese in his ancestry.

been blue and tan, grizzle, or wheaten in color. The Clydesdale was a blue and tan terrier, weighing up to 18 pounds (8.3 kg), and the Paisley was a smaller dog, weighing up to 12 pounds (5.4 kg), with a lighter blue coat. These dogs were highly valued for their ability to scare off vermin, and they were used in homes and in workplaces to keep mice and rats at bay.

Inevitably, these Scottish terriers interbred with native dogs in Lancashire and Yorkshire. These would have included the Manchester Terrier, the Black and Tan Terrier, the Halifax Fawn, and the Silky Terrier. It is fair to say that all these breeds played a part in creating the Yorkshire Terrier. It is even thought that the exotic Maltese may have been interbred at a later date, to improve the Yorkie coat.

DESIGNER DOGS

What was needed was a small, fearless dog to keep vermin under control. Even better, was a dog that was such a good ratter that he could compete in ratting contests, while the owners gambled on the outcome.

The ratting recordbreaker of his day was a dog called Billy, who killed 100 rats in a pit in just seven and a half minutes. A Yorkshire Terrier of about 6 pounds (2.7 kg) was recorded as killing 20 large rats in three minutes – an amazing feat for such a small dog. This is the unlikely background of the world's most glamorous Toy dog, and anyone who knows the breed can still see signs of the tenacious little terrier, who was brave enough to take on a roomful of rats.

It was not long before the canny Yorkshiremen found another use for their dogs. The first formally organized dog shows began in England in 1859, and it was the miniature dogs that attracted the most attention, both in the ring, and then with a growing demand for pet dogs. At that time, most Yorkshire Terriers weighed between 12 and 15 pounds (5.4 and 8 kg), but they were soon bred down to a more fashionable size. A typical Yorkie was shown at around 8–10 pounds (3.6–4.5 kg), and later it was not unusual for dogs to be as small as 3–5 pounds (1.4–2.3 kg).

The real credit for inventing the Yorkshire Terrier as a breed in its own right goes to Peter Eden of Manchester. He was a highly respected terrier breeder, and he judged at many of the shows run by the newly-formed Kennel Club. He had a number of successful dogs, with long, silky blue and tan coats. It was his dog, Albert, that gained entry in the first Kennel Club Stud Book under the heading of "Broken Haired Scotch and Yorkshire Terriers."

HUDDERSFIELD BEN

It is a fact that nearly every Yorkie can trace its origins back to Huddersfield Ben. This dog was born in 1865, and was bred by Mr. Eastwood of Huddersfield, Yorkshire. Huddersfield Ben was well bred – Albert, who first gained entry to the Kennel Club Stud Book, is featured on both sides of his pedigree. He made his debut in the show ring where he was entered as a Scotch Terrier, and won second prize. This was the start of a glittering show career.

The Yorkie has moved a long way from his rat-catching past.

Tragically, Huddersfield Ben was killed in a road accident when he was only six years old, but, in his short life, he left an indelible mark on the breed. His show wins meant that he was in great demand as a stud dog, and it was soon discovered that he had the ability to pass on his outstanding qualities to many of his offspring. In total, 30 of his progeny were registered in the Kennel Club Stud Book.

TRANSATLANTIC LINKS

The Yorkshire Terrier soon established itself as a

The breed has grown in popularity and now enjoys a worldwide fan club.

firm favorite in the show ring and among pet owners, and its reputation spread outside Britain. In 1880, the first Yorkshire Terrier was exported to the U.S., and the first Yorkie to gain his American title was an English export called Bradford Harry – a grandson of the great Huddersfield Ben.

The breed grew in popularity on both sides of the Atlantic, and influential bloodlines were developed to ensure the future well-being of the breed.

Today, the Yorkie has a worldwide fan club, both as a pet and as a show dog. In the U.S., the Yorkshire Terrier ranks as the sixth most popular breed, with annual registrations of around 42,000. In the U.K., the Yorkie is eleventh in the ratings, with registrations of around 5,000 a year.

THE VERSATILE YORKIE

The Yorkshire Terrier's ratting history is long since buried, and the breed's prime role is as a companion and as a show dog. However, it would be wrong to think that the Yorkie is a "pin-up" dog, relying on his beauty rather than his brains.

The Yorkie has a keen intelligence, and he is happy to put this to good use. He has made his mark in competitive Obedience, and his speed has stood him in good stead in the demanding world of Agility. The new sport of Freestyle (Heelwork to Music) is tailormade for a dog that loves to be in the limelight.

Despite his small size, the Yorkie is also proving his worth as an assistance dog. Representatives of the breed work as hearing dogs for deaf people, and the sweet, affectionate side of the Yorkie is ideal for therapy work, where dogs bring comfort to those in residential care.

Regardless of his many talents and his beautiful looks, the Yorkshire Terrier stands apart as the ideal companion dog. He is wonderfully entertaining – there is never a dull moment when a Yorkie is about – and he is also loyal and loving. This is a dog that is ready to give so much, and that asks for so little in return.

If you take on a Yorkshire Terrier, do not treat him like a fragile toy – treat him like a proper dog. Give him the diet and exercise he needs, look after his coat, and give him the mental stimulation that is so important to this bright, intelligent, little dog, and you will be rewarded a thousandfold.

CHAPTER TWO

PUPPY POWER

The Yorkshire Terrier is one of the most captivating breeds, and Yorkie puppies are second to none. There is something about their cheeky, mischievous expression, and ragamuffin looks that is irresistible. It is tempting to think that it will be no problem to look after a small Toy dog – but you would be wise to think long and hard before embarking on Yorkie ownership. You will be responsible for a living creature for the duration of his life, and there are a number of important points you will need to consider:

• **Can you give a Yorkie the companionship he requires?** This is a breed that thrives on human company, and a Yorkie will be miserable if he is left for long periods on his own. No dog, of any breed, should be left on his own for longer than four hours a day.

• **Can you afford to keep a dog?** Toy dogs do not cost much to feed, but there are additional expenses, such as veterinary bills and boarding fees if you need to kennel your dog while you go away.

• **Do you have small children?** Most Yorkie breeders do not like to sell a pup to a family that has children under the age of eight. This is not the result of downright prejudice – it is undeniable that tiny Toy dogs and small children are not a good mix. A ten-week-old Yorkie pup is in serious danger of being injured if he is roughly handled, and it is simply not worth taking the risk. However, if you have older children, and they are taught how to behave around dogs, there is no reason why a Yorkie should not make an excellent family companion (see page 29).

• **Do you have other dogs at home?** If you already have a Yorkie, you will have little cause for concern, particularly if you opt for a dog of the opposite sex. If you own a large breed of dog, you must be prepared to supervise initial interactions until the dogs learn to accept each other (see page 31).

The adult Yorkie has a glorious coat, but it takes a huge amount of work to keep a dog in full coat.

- **Are you prepared to spend time training and socializing a Yorkie?** An owner is not only responsible for routine care; a dog must also be thoroughly trained and socialized to be a well-behaved canine citizen (see pages 43 and 47).

- **Are you prepared to cope with the Yorkshire Terrier's coat?** You may have seen show dogs looking unbelievably glamorous, but the long, flowing, tanglefree coat is the result of hours of hard work. It requires incredible dedication to keep a Yorkie in full coat, and if you are a newcomer to the breed, you should find out exactly what this entails (see page 72). The option is to clip your Yorkie, which can look smart and attractive. However, this does not mean that the workload disappears. A Yorkie still needs to be groomed every day, and will require bathing at least once every two weeks. You will also need to budget for having your Yorkie clipped approximately every three months.

- **Are you fit enough to look after a dog?** Many elderly people opt for a Toy breed because exercise requirements are moderate, but you still need to be able to take your Yorkie out and about in order to give him an interesting and varied life.

- **Are you prepared to care for a Yorkie for the duration of his life?** This is a long-lived breed that may well carry on to his teens – some even make it to their late teens and early twenties. This may well seem unimportant when you are considering buying a puppy, but it is important to plan for the future, particularly if you are getting on in years.

Take time to weigh all the pros and cons, and if you are still anxious to take on a Yorkie, you will probably find that it is the best decision you ever made. This is a breed that really gets under your skin, and Yorkie owners must rank as among the most enthusiastic and dedicated of all dog owners.

WHERE TO START

Now that you have decided that the Yorkshire Terrier is the breed for you, the next step is to find the perfect puppy! Do not make the mistake of rushing out to the nearest pet store, or checking out the advertisements in your local paper in the hope of finding a litter of puppies nearby. It is such a big decision to take on a dog, you should ensure that you get exactly what you want.

Take time to read some books about the breed; you will also find special videos available. Surf the Internet and investigate some of the Yorkie web sites, and go to some dog shows where you can look at the breed first hand. As you find out more about the breed, you will also start to develop an eye for the type of Yorkie that you like. Obviously, a Yorkshire Terrier looks like a Yorkshire Terrier, but you will start to see subtle differences in the stock produced by different breeders, and you can

Take time to find a reputable breeder of Yorkshire Terriers.

decide which type of Yorkie you would like to own. This is highly significant if you plan to show your Yorkie, but even if you just want a Yorkie as a companion, there is no reason why you should not be selective.

You can approach breeders at a show, through special dog papers/magazines, or through the Internet. You can also contact your national kennel club, and find out about the breed clubs in your area. In most cases, the breed club secretary will know which breeders have puppies for sale. It is essential that you only approach breeders whose dogs are registered with your kennel club. In this way, you can be totally confident that you are buying a purebred puppy, and hopefully, the breeder will have a longstanding reputation that he/she will be eager to preserve.

VISITING THE LITTER

Generally, Yorkshire Terrier puppies are ready to go to their new homes at around 10-12 weeks of age, but you will be able to view the litter before that date. Each breeder will have his/her own policy as to when you can see the puppies, but, in most cases, you should be able to visit at around eight weeks of age. By this time, the puppies will be up on their feet, and you will get some idea of their looks and personality.

If you are choosing a puppy to show, it is advisable to wait until the puppies are between 12-16 weeks of age so that you are better able to assess coat and conformation.

When you visit a litter, check out the following:

• Are the premises clean and fresh-smelling?
• Are the adult Yorkies friendly and welcoming?
• Do the puppies look well cared for?
• Is the mother happy to show off her babies?

In most cases, the litter will be reared in the breeder's home, and this is certainly an advantage. The puppies will be used to the sights and sounds of a busy household, and will have been handled and socialized from the very earliest stage.

It is important to see the mother with her puppies, as this will give you some idea of her temperament, and how the puppies may turn out. It is unlikely that you will see the puppies' father, as, in most cases, he will be standing at stud with another breeder. However, the breeder should be able to show you a photo of him, and give you details of his health, temperament, possibly his show career, and of the puppies he has produced to date.

It will be helpful if you can meet adult Yorkies that are closely related to the litter of puppies you have come to view. This will give you an impression of the type of dogs that are being produced by the kennel, and, just as importantly, you will be able to assess their temperament.

You should also check that both the mother and the father of the puppies are clear of inherited disorders. Fortunately, the Yorkshire Terrier is a healthy breed, but you should check that the line you are planning to buy into is free from breed-specific problems, such as slipping

It is important to see the mother with her puppies.

patellas and incorrect dentition (see Chapter Nine: Health Care).

You should also find out if the breeder provides an after-sales advice service. All responsible breeders are only too happy to offer help if asked, particularly if you are new to Yorkie ownership. In most cases, the breeder will also offer to take the dog back, at any stage in his life, if you are no longer able to provide a suitable home. If you are happy with the answers to all your questions, you can start to examine the puppies in more detail.

- They should appear plump, but not pot-bellied, as the latter could be an indication of worm infestation.
- Their eyes should be clear and bright, with no evidence of discharge from either the eyes or the nose.
- The rear ends should be clean – a dirty rear could indicate the pup is suffering from diarrhea.
- The puppies should be lively and inquisitive, and be eager to come up and meet you.

SIZE MATTERS

You will almost certainly notice a difference in size between the littermates. This is because the Yorkshire Terrier is a man-made breed (see Chapter One: Introducing the Yorkshire Terrier), and even though it has been around for nearly 200 years, it does not always breed true. This means that there is variety within the breed, particularly when it comes to size. In an average litter, puppies may develop into adults that weigh as much as 9 pounds (4.1 kg) or as little as 3 pounds (1.4 kg).

If you have plans to show your dog, you do not want a big, chunky puppy. The weight limit is set at 7 pounds (3.2 kg) for both males and females. However, a medium to large puppy is likely to be more robust than a tiny specimen, and so this could be a good option for a pet home. The variation in weight between puppies is evident at birth, although you can be surprised by a smaller puppy having a growth spurt, or equally, a bigger puppy can slow down. However, by the time the puppies are between 10-12 weeks, a breeder will have a pretty good idea of how big a puppy will grow.

There is often a discernible difference in size between littermates.

DOCKING

By tradition, a Yorkie has a docked tail, and this simple procedure is usually carried out by a veterinarian when the puppies are around four days old. However, there is increasing opposition to docking, and it is now banned in a number of European countries. At the moment, it is customary for tails to be docked in the U.K. and in the U.S., but there is growing pressure for this situation to change (see page 99). At present, if you want a Yorkie with a full tail, you will need to find a breeder who specializes in breeding pet dogs.

TURNING THE TABLES

While you are assessing the puppies, the breeder will probably be assessing you! A responsible breeder will ask lots of questions to find out if a potential owner can provide a suitable home. You will be asked about your family, your work commitments, and about your future plans. The breeder is not prying; it is his job to ensure that the puppies he has reared go to the best possible homes.

MAKING A CHOICE

The average number of puppies in a Yorkie litter is three to four. But it is not unusual for the litter to contain just one puppy, or there could be as many as eight puppies.

You would be wise to allow the breeder to help you to choose a puppy. The breeder has had the advantage of watching the puppies closely over a period of time, and will have an intimate knowledge of their individual personalities.

Some breeders carry out temperament tests so that they can make a more thorough assessment of each puppy. For example, a bold, extrovert puppy, that is always the first to come forward and shows little fear, is more likely to fit in with a family that has children than the shy, retiring type that needs that extra bit of reassurance.

MALE OR FEMALE?

This is largely a matter of personal preference, particularly if you want a companion Yorkie and you have no plans to breed from your dog.

Many pet owners opt for a female, believing that she will be less trouble than a male. However, you must bear in mind that a female Yorkie comes into season approximately every eight months, and you will have to keep her away from male dogs for a three-week period, or you could risk an unplanned mating. You can

The breeder will help you choose a pup that is most likely to fit in with your lifestyle.

In terms of temperament, it is almost impossible to pick out characteristics that are more typically male, or more typically female. This is a breed that is full of individuals, and you could get a quiet, laid-back male, and a dominant, outgoing female, or it could, just as easily, be the other way around. The one generalization that seems to be true is that male dogs have a preference for female owners, and females prefer male owners.

DOUBLE TROUBLE

Yorkie puppies are irresistible, and there are many owners who have gone out to buy one puppy and come back with two!

This can work out fine, as long as you are prepared to give each puppy individual training

Two pups will certainly double your workload.

use a specially manufactured spray to disguise your bitch's scent at this time, but she will still need to be kept away from the neighborhood Romeos.

If you choose a male, you will not have a seasonal cycle to cope with, but a mature male will have certain traits, such as cocking his leg to mark his territory. A well-trained dog will quickly learn that this is undesirable behavior in the house, but you will need to keep a close eye on him if there are bitches in season living nearby, as he may have a tendency to roam.

If you are not planning to breed or exhibit your Yorkie in the show ring, you may be advised to consider the benefits of neutering (see page 66).

and socialization. You may also find that the puppies are more orientated toward each other than to their human family. If you take on two puppies, it is always best to go for opposite sexes. This is also true if you already have a dog at home.

A male and female Yorkie seem to get on especially well, and there is no rivalry between them. If you have two males or two females, you often find that one of the dogs becomes more dominant, and the other suffers as a result.

Of course, if you have a mixed pair, you must be aware of the danger of an unplanned mating unless you decide to neuter.

SHOW PROSPECT

If you are planning to show your Yorkie, you must inform the breeder of your intentions. It is a mistake to think that you will get a bargain if you keep your plans quiet by saying that you only want a pet Yorkie, and then hoping you can show your dog at a later stage.

Showing is highly competitive, and only the very best specimens of the breed will make their mark in the ring. A breeder has a reputation to guard, and would be most unhappy if a puppy that was sold as a pet ended up in the ring. That is not to say that there is anything wrong with a Yorkie that is sold as a pet. The puppy will probably be a good specimen of the breed with the typical Yorkie temperament. However, he will not possess the finer points of perfection that are required when competing at the top level (see Chapter Eight: Seeking Perfection).

AN OLDER DOG

You may feel that you cannot cope with taking on a puppy, and an older dog would be more suitable. If this is the case, you may be lucky enough to find that a Yorkie breeder has older dogs available. Often, a breeder will hold onto a couple of puppies to see how they mature. By the time the puppies are nearly grown, the breeder will decide whether they are suitable for the show ring.

If a youngster does not turn out to have the top-quality coat, conformation, and movement, which are required for showing, he may be sold as a pet. Equally, a breeder may decide to retire a Yorkie from the show ring, or from breeding, and such a dog may benefit from going to a pet home rather than being kept in a kennel full of Yorkies.

If you decide to take on an adult, you will have to work hard during the settling-in period, as an older dog will take longer to adapt to a new home. However, if you work at building up your Yorkie's trust, you will be rewarded with many years of happy companionship.

Taking on an older dog may be a better choice in some circumstances.

Unfortunately, far too many Yorkies end up in rescue shelters. In many cases, this is through no fault of the dog. An owner may become ill and be unable to cope with a dog, or sometimes an elderly owner dies, and there is no one left to care for the pet. Marital breakup is also responsible for pet Yorkies losing their homes.

If you decide to take on a rescued dog, you should be aware of the problems that may be involved. It is very traumatic for an adult dog to lose his owner, and it will take time before he will be ready to trust his new family.

Beryl Evans has been involved with Yorkshire Terrier rescue for over 20 years. Currently, she works as rescue coordinator for the Yorkshire Terrier Club in the U.K. She figures that between 500-600 Yorkies are rehomed every year. Interestingly, she has noticed a change in circumstances of dogs that need rehoming.

"When I first got involved in rescue, we had a lot of dogs that had been bred in puppy farms (puppy mills)," said Beryl. "They were often unsound in temperament, or scarcely looked like Yorkshire Terriers at all, and their owners didn't want anything more to do with them. Now, we rarely get Yorkies from this source. Elderly owners who have to go into residential care account for a fair number, but marital breakup accounts for many more.

"Increasingly, we get people who decide to take a job abroad, and decide they cannot take their dog with them. Sadly, Yorkies also seem to be victims of our disposable society, and dogs end up in rescue because their owners have lost interest in them, or they want to work full-time

A rescued dog has a lot of love to give.

and the dog has become a nuisance."

Fortunately, there are many people who are eager to rehome Yorkies, and Beryl gets as many as 15 inquiries a day. Applicants are carefully interviewed, as many people do not appreciate the work that is involved in settling an adult Yorkie into a new home.

"I always say that taking on a rescued dog is like taking on a two-year-old child," said Beryl. "The dog knows what life is all about, but he doesn't understand why. For a dog like a Yorkie, that loves being with people, it is hugely traumatic to lose a home and family at one time. Some dogs take a long time to readjust. I may have an owner calling up after three months to say the dog is still failing to adjust, whereas I could get someone telling me that the dog was perfectly at home within a week. All dogs are different, and they need to be treated as individuals, with patience and understanding."

A SPECIAL KIND OF CARING

Iris Pethic and her husband, Geoffrey, who live in Worcestershire, England, decided that they wanted to give a home to an older Yorkshire Terrier – the type of dog that is hardest to rehome. Their generosity has been rewarded with the very special relationships they have had with their rescued dogs.

"Penny was our first Yorkie," said Iris. "She was 15 years old when we got her, and she was virtually a cripple. But she was a most endearing character, and we loved her dearly for the two years that were left to her.

"We were then put in touch with the Yorkshire Terrier Club rescue, and we were told that a dog called Sophie might suit us. We went to meet her, but that very morning a new dog had arrived from Essex. We were met by lots of Yorkshire Terriers, and one little dog jumped up onto the sofa to sit with us. This was Amy, and I think it was fate that decided she was to be our dog.

"We did not know her age, or anything about her background, but she settled in with us as if she had never known another home. She was a quiet little soul, with a very gentle side to her character. I work as an aromatherapist, and Amy started to sit with me while I was working. She was a

Penny enjoyed two happy years in her new home.

THE WAITING GAME

You will probably have at least a couple of weeks to wait before the Yorkie puppy you have chosen is ready to take home. This may seem frustrating, but your puppy will benefit from the extra time he spends with his littermates. He will be stronger and more ready to adapt to life on his own if he is given that little bit of extra time in his first home. Some breeders suggest that you provide some bedding for your new puppy, which he can start using in the weeks before he is ready to go home. This will mean that he has something familiar to take with him, and it will help to ease the transition between homes.

The breeder may register names for the puppies with your national kennel club (in the U.S., this is most often the American Kennel Club, in the U.K. it is the Kennel Club), which will include the breeder's kennel name. This is important in the show world, as it identifies all puppies that bear the kennel name as coming from a particular breeder. However, your puppy will need his own pet name, and if you make a decision at an early stage, the breeder can start calling your puppy by companion to me, but she also helped by being with the patients. Because of this, I trained her to become a therapy dog, working with me in a unit for cancer patients. Amy gave so much love, she was a real comfort to the dying. Tragically, she also became a victim of cancer, and we lost her after just two years.

"Our grief was eventually eased with the arrival of Poppy, a lively, three-year-old Yorkie. She did not have a good start to her life; she was kept in a crate for long periods and she was teased a lot. As a result, she is rather nervous and high strung, but she is learning to trust us now. She is completely different from Amy; she is very lively and full of fun. She likes to play all sorts of games. We have given her lots of attention, and have been patient with her so that she has had the chance to build up her confidence gradually.

"She sits with me when I am working, and I think she benefits from the calm atmosphere. She gets on well with my patients, but I think she is too nervous to become a therapy dog. We have thought about getting another Yorkie to keep her company, but she is made so much of, I think she may resent a companion.

"She is Queen of the May here, and that is how it should be!"

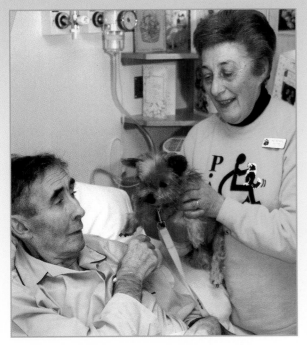

Amy's sensitivity made her an ideal therapy dog.

his new name, so that he will respond to it by the time you are ready to take him home.

BUYING EQUIPMENT

While you are waiting to collect your puppy, you can spend the time getting everything ready for him. Fortunately, dogs do not need a huge amount of equipment, but there are a number of essential items.

Bed

Your puppy will need a cozy bed to sleep in. To begin with, this can be a cardboard box, lined with bedding. Make sure you remove all metal staples from the box, and cut down the front so that your puppy can get in and out of the box without difficulty. The advantage of providing a temporary bed is that it does not matter if it is chewed or soiled – you can simply throw it away and start again.

There is a huge variety of different dog beds, and the type you choose is largely a matter of personal choice. The most practical option is a hard plastic bed, which can be lined with

Your pup will need a cozy bed to sleep in.

bedding. This type of bed is fairly indestructible, and is also easy to clean. They come in a wide range of sizes, so that you can buy a bed that is tailormade for an adult Yorkie.

If you buy a cushion-type bed, make sure the cover can be removed for washing. If you prefer to buy a soft, fabric bed, you would be advised to wait until your puppy is around six months old and has gotten beyond the chewing phase.

Bedding

You can use an old blanket to line the bed, but in terms of convenience, you cannot beat the synthetic fleece bedding that is made especially for dogs. This is warm and cozy; it is machine-washable, and dries quickly. The best plan is to buy two pieces of bedding, so that you can have one in use, and one as a spare.

Crate/Carrier

This is the most expensive item of equipment you will need to buy, but it is well worth the investment. You can buy a purpose-built crate, which you can use at home and in the car, or you can buy a carrier, which can be dual-purpose, providing accommodation at home, as well as being a means of transporting your Yorkie (see page 44).

The crate you buy should be double the length of an adult Yorkie, and at least one-and-a-half times the dog's height. If you are buying a carrier that will only be used for traveling, it can be a little smaller.

The great advantage of using a crate/carrier is that you can provide a secure place for your Yorkie when you are not able to supervise him. The crate/carrier should be lined with soft bedding, and you will need to spend time introducing your puppy to it so that he does not feel he is being shut in and abandoned. For information on crate training, see page 35.

You will find that a dog that is used to being in a crate looks on it as his own special den. He will go in there of his own accord when the door is left open, and will relish a bit of peace and quiet. If you go away from home, you can take the crate with you, so your Yorkie has his very own home away from home.

Dog bowls

You will need two bowls: one for water and one for food. There are plenty of different types to choose from, but if you want something that will last, you would be advised to go for the stainless steel type. These come in lots of different sizes, and they are easy to clean. Plastic bowls look bright and cheerful, but they can be chewed. Some owners like to buy a heavy, ceramic bowl for drinking water. This type of bowl is too heavy to be picked up by a mischievous puppy, but it is breakable.

Collar and lead

You will need to buy a collar and lead for your puppy. Remember the size of your Yorkie puppy, and get a small, lightweight collar, which will not be too cumbersome for the tiny pup. The lead should also be fine, but make sure it has a secure trigger fastening.

Identification

When your Yorkie has completed his vaccination course (see page 114), and is old enough to go out in public places, he will need to have a form of identification. Identification can take the form of a tag attached to your dog's collar and engraved with your contact details, or it can be a more permanent form of identity, such as an ear tattoo or a microchip implant. If you plan to use a permanent form of identification, you can discuss the procedure with your veterinarian, but a collar tag will still be needed in addition to this.

Grooming gear

If you have chosen a Yorkshire Terrier, you will realize that grooming is a huge part of caring for this glamorous breed. Coat care must start from day one, and so it is important that you have the correct gear to care for your puppy's coat.

Although the workload increases as the Yorkie's coat grows, the same basic equipment is needed for puppy and adult grooming. You will need a soft, bristle brush, and a wide-toothed comb. Be extra careful when you are buying a comb – the tips of the teeth should not be too sharp or too pointed. This type of comb could easily damage the Yorkie's coat, or it could scratch the skin, causing considerable discomfort. For detailed information on grooming see page 72.

Clean up!

Every responsible owner must clean up after his/her dog if he fouls in a public place. This is not the most attractive aspect of owning a dog, but it is an essential part of keeping a dog in the community. The anti-dog lobby, who try to ban dogs from an increasing number of public places, should not be given additional ammunition. Your local pet store will sell clean-up bags or pooper scoops – so make sure you are always equipped when you take your Yorkshire Terrier out.

Food

In most cases, the breeder will supply you with enough food to last for the first couple of days after your pup has arrived home. However, it would be a good idea to find out what diet the puppy is used to, and to get in a supply.

You may decide to change the diet in due course, particularly if you have trouble getting hold of a particular brand, but you should ensure that the puppy does not have to cope with a change of diet in the first couple of weeks of arriving home. For information on feeding your puppy, see page 37.

Toys

This is the fun part of the shopping list – and you will be amazed at the choice of toys that are made especially for dogs. You can buy squeaky toys, hard, rubber, chew toys, and tug toys made of rope.

You can buy whatever takes your fancy – as long as you check that they are 100 percent safe. A chewing puppy – even one the size of a Yorkshire Terrier – can reduce a toy to shreds, and this can be potentially lethal if small pieces are swallowed.

Make sure the toys you buy for your puppy are 100 percent safe.

PREPARING YOUR HOME

If you have never owned a puppy before, you could be fooled into thinking that a tiny Yorkie pup is not going to make much impact on your home. Think again! The Yorkie may be small, but he is lionhearted, and he has a mission to explore everything, even if it towers above him.

Try to look at your house from a puppy's perspective, and imagine what he is likely to find fascinating: curtains that reach to the floor, mats and furnishings with fringes, a tablecloth that hangs close to floor level, an arrangement of dried flowers, a shelf full of books… the list is endless. It is not only a matter of preserving your home; you also need to protect your puppy from his own curiosity. A trailing electric cord or a poisonous houseplant all seem fair game to a puppy with an inquisitive mind.

There are two ways to puppy-proof your home. First, try to remove anything that is valuable or potentially harmful out of a puppy's reach. As your puppy matures and becomes more civilized, you can return to your former arrangements, but, for the first few months, the motto is: better safe than sorry.

The second line of defense is to decide where your puppy is allowed to go, and to exclude him from certain areas of the house. For example, you may decide that you do not want your puppy to go upstairs, or you want to keep him out of the living room until he is fully house-trained. This can be achieved by installing a stairgate (child gate) at the bottom of the stairs, or in the doorway between two rooms. Your puppy will quickly learn that the gate signals a no-go zone, and he will be content to stay in his permitted area. In fact, this teaches your puppy an important lesson in learning to

Look on the garden as your puppy's playground.

cope on his own, and will prevent separation anxiety from developing (see page 65).

You will also need to decide where your puppy is going to sleep. Many owners opt for the kitchen or utility room, but it is largely a matter of personal convenience. It is important that the sleeping area is warm in the winter, cool in hot weather, and is free from drafts.

If you are planning to use a crate, you can find a place for the crate in the kitchen, and put a dog bed in the sitting room, so that your Yorkie has his own place to go when the family is sitting together, talking, or watching television.

THE YARD

Until your puppy is fully vaccinated, you will not be able to take him into the outside world. The yard will therefore be a very important place: it will be his playground and his toilet area. As your puppy grows up, he will continue to enjoy spending time in the yard, so it is essential to ensure that it is a safe environment.

The first priority is to check the fencing, and to make sure the gate has a secure fastening. Yorkshire Terriers are great escapologists, and many a Yorkie has dug or climbed his way to freedom. Ideally, the fencing should be 4-5 feet (1.2-1.5 meters) in height, but it is the bottom 2 feet (0.6 meters) that are of vital importance. Fencing should be 100 percent secure, and it should be solid. This is particularly important if your neighbor has a cat or a dog, as your Yorkie could easily get obsessed with running along the fence and barking every time he thinks something is going on in the next-door yard.

If you store pesticides in a garden shed, you must make sure that the door fastens securely. Equally, you should check out all the chemicals you use in the yard, and make sure they are safe to use if you have a dog. There are some plants that are poisonous to dogs – ask for advice at your garden center.

It is a good idea to allocate an area in the yard that your puppy can use for toileting purposes. This will help the process of house-training, and it will make cleaning up easier.

FINDING A VETERINARIAN

If you do not already have a dog, you will need to register with a veterinarian in your area. If your Yorkie's breeder lives locally, you can ask for a recommendation, or you can ask friends in the area who own dogs. If you cannot find a veterinarian through personal recommendation, you will need to look through the telephone directory, and then make an appointment to visit the practice that seems most suitable.

Find out the answers to the following questions:

• Is there a veterinarian in the practice that has experience in treating Toy dogs, and ideally Yorkshire Terriers?

• What facilities are available (e.g., X-ray, ultrasound, etc.).

• What are the arrangements for emergencies?

• If you are interested, ask if alternative therapies, such as homoeopathy, are available.

If you are happy with the answers to your questions, make an appointment so your veterinarian can give your puppy a thorough checkup a few days after he has arrived in his new home.

The inquisitive Yorkie will explore every nook and cranny of his new surroundings.

GETTING YOUR PUPPY

At last the waiting is over, and it is time to get your puppy. The best plan is to travel with one other adult, so someone can concentrate on driving while the other looks after the puppy.

You can bring a carrier, lined with bedding, for your puppy to travel home in. However, on this one occasion, the puppy will probably settle better if he is cuddled on a lap. Take some bedding or a towel for the puppy to lie on, and some paper towels in case of accidents. If you have a long journey, or it is a hot day, you will need to take a bowl and some fresh drinking water.

Try to arrange to get your puppy as early in the morning as possible, so that you have the maximum amount of time at home with your puppy before you have to settle him for the night.

Puppy pack

The breeder will have prepared a puppy pack, so that you have all the relevant information about your puppy on hand. It should include:

- Kennel club registration documents, including a form for the transfer of ownership.
- Your puppy's pedigree.
- Details of any inoculations.
- Details of his worming program to date, and when the next treatment is due.
- A diet sheet, giving information on the type of food the puppy is used to, and the quantity he should be given.
- A sample of food for the first couple of days.
- Contact details so that you can be given help and advice if necessary.

At long last it is time to introduce your puppy to his new home.

Hopefully, your puppy will quickly settle down on the journey home, although he will probably make a token protest. Try not to break up your trip.

If you have to stop, remember your puppy is not fully vaccinated – he must not go on the ground in case other dogs have been exercised in the area.

CHAPTER THREE

SETTLING IN

Just imagine how your puppy feels when he first arrives in his new home. He has been taken away from his brothers and sisters and all that is familiar to him. He has traveled in a car with strange people, and now he finds himself in a completely new environment. Nothing looks the same or smells the same, and worse still, he has to face everything on his own. This is, without doubt, the most traumatic time in a dog's life, so you must work hard to give your puppy the reassurance he so desperately needs.

ARRIVING HOME

When you first arrive home, take your puppy into the backyard. Go to the area you have designated for toileting and, when your puppy relieves himself, give lots of praise (see House-training, page 36). Before you go into the house, let the puppy explore his new surroundings. He will probably be very tentative, so be ready to encourage him and give him confidence.

When you go into the house, take your puppy to his sleeping area, and show him his bed. If you want to use a crate, you can introduce him to it (see Crate-training, page 35).

Allow your puppy to look around and investigate, without overwhelming him with too much attention. He needs a chance to get used to his new surroundings.

MEETING THE FAMILY

It is tempting to ask all your friends and neighbors around to meet the new arrival – but it is best to avoid this for a few days. Your little Yorkie is trying to find out who he belongs to, and so it is unfair to confuse him with lots of different people. Let him meet each member of the family in turn, so that he gets used to their different smells and voices. Do not rush him at this stage – your puppy wants the chance to get to know everyone, rather than becoming a canine version of pass the package.

Do not overwhelm your puppy with too many visitors.

INTRODUCING CHILDREN

The Yorkshire Terrier is an excellent addition to a family with children, as long as the children and the puppy learn to respect each other. This is essential whatever type of dog you choose, but when you are dealing with a tiny puppy, children must understand that he is not a toy that can be picked up and played with at will.

- Start by getting your child/children to sit on the floor. It is much safer to conduct all interactions at floor level, as this minimizes the danger of the puppy being dropped.
- Give each of the children a treat, and then allow each child to hold the puppy, cuddle him, and give him a treat.

- You can then get some toys out, and let each child have a little play with the puppy.
- Make sure the children remain calm and do not shout or scream. This may be the first time the puppy has met children, and so it is important that he does not feel frightened or become too hyped up.

For the first few days, supervise all interactions so that both the children and the puppy learn how to behave. If the following rules are observed, your Yorkie will quickly become integrated in family life.

- The children must be careful when the puppy is running around – particularly in the yard. When children are busy playing a game, it is easy to step on a paw by mistake.
- Do not allow the children to pick up the puppy and walk around with him, as he could struggle and fall.
- Discourage rough-and-tumble games, and games of tug. A Yorkie puppy may well be eager to join in, but it will inevitably lead to trouble.
- The puppy must not be disturbed when he is sleeping or eating.
- The puppy must not nip the children when he is playing with them. It is easy to dismiss this behavior as harmless puppy behavior, but he must learn that biting is always unacceptable.
- If your puppy has a tendency to nip, practice giving him treats, and use the word "Gently" when he takes the treat without grabbing it. If the puppy attempts to bite, withhold the treat until he is ready to take it properly. When your

A FAMILY AFFAIR

Donna Hayden's three children were teenagers when her first Yorkie, Gemma, joined the family. That was the start of a passion for the breed that has now spread to her grandchildren.

"We always had dogs in the family before Gemma arrived, so the children knew how to behave around dogs," said Donna. "Our dogs were mostly working terriers, so a Yorkshire Terrier was quite a change. However, the same principles apply in terms of teaching the children to respect the dog and to be sensible. In fact, Gemma was very good with the children, and she was an ideal family pet."

Gemma was bought as a companion, but soon Donna became captivated by the breed and she started her own show kennel. Donna's daughter took an interest in the new venture, but it is her grandchildren that have become the great enthusiasts.

"Sheralee was keen on the Yorkies ever since she was tiny," said Donna. "She helped me with my dogs, and soon she was taking them into the ring for me. I gave her a puppy, called Emma (Donahaye Delightful Charm), for

Jade with the Yorkie she has just started to show.

her birthday, and when she was just 14, she became the youngest handler to win a Challenge Certificate and Best of Breed."

Sheralee is now 19, and she has started her own kennel, using the My Sherie affix. At the moment her youngster, My Sherie Royal Romance, is Top Puppy in the breed. She is still helping Donna with her dogs. She handled Ch. Donahaye Double Delight when he won the CC and Best of Breed at Crufts (U.K.) 2000, and she is always ready to help with the up-and-coming show prospects.

"Sheralee is a fantastic handler," said Donna. "If I am bringing on a couple of dogs at the same time, it makes sense to hand one of them over to her. We like to help each other out whenever we can."

The family connection does not end with Sheralee. Her younger sister, Jade, aged nine, is passionately interested in the breed, and has already started showing dogs in the ring. Jade qualified the puppy she is handling for Crufts and another major show.

"It's the beauty of the breed that gets us," said Donna. "They are also wonderful dogs to live with – we would never be without them."

puppy has learned the command "Gently," you can use it in a variety of situations, such as when your puppy is playing with his toys.

THE RESIDENT DOG

If you already have a dog, you will be anxious that relations with the new puppy get off to a good start. The best plan is to take your puppy and the resident dog into the backyard, so they can meet on relatively neutral territory. Unless you are really worried about the adult dog's reaction, it is better if he is allowed off the lead, as he will not feel pressured. Dogs have their own method of communicating, and it is far better to allow the adult and puppy to meet without human interference, so they can sort out their own relationship.

To begin with, the adult will sniff the puppy, and the puppy will almost certainly show that he is submissive. He will do this by flattening his ears and licking the adult's mouth; he may even roll over onto his back. A good-natured adult will generally respond with lots of tail wagging, and may even instigate a game. If your puppy is a bit bold, the adult may give a warning growl. This is perfectly natural; it is the adult's way of asserting his authority. It means: "Watch out" – it does not mean that the puppy is about to be attacked. Stand back, and allow the puppy and adult to interact, and give the adult lots of praise when he is nice to the puppy.

Supervise all interaction between the two dogs for the first few days, and you will soon find that they establish their own relationship with each other. Remember, it is easy for the adult dog to feel slightly put out when a new puppy arrives, so make sure you do not focus all your attention on the puppy. At this stage, the puppy will not be able to go out for walks, so you can use this time to make a big fuss over your adult dog, and spend some quality time together.

To begin with, the adult dog will assume superior status over the puppy, but this may well change as your puppy matures. Again, it is best to allow the two dogs to sort things out between them rather than trying to take sides. Once the two dogs have decided who is the

Yorkies mix well with dogs of all breeds.

boss, you will find that there is no further cause for concern. Unlike humans, dogs accept the status quo and will very rarely challenge it.

FELINE RELATIONS

It is important to bear in mind that although the Yorkie is classed as a Toy dog, he is a terrier at heart. This means that he is fearless and persistent, and if you are not careful, he may think a cat is fair game for chasing. You must not allow this situation to develop. To begin with, your puppy will be much smaller, and he will be very vulnerable to being attacked. A cat under threat will not think twice about striking out with sharp claws, and this could lead to serious injury. Equally, you do not want your cat to spend the rest of her life being terrorized by a small but determined Yorkshire Terrier.

To get relations off on the right footing, try the following:

THE SMALLEST T-REX

Peggy and Bill Seiler live in Marion, Texas. They own two Yorkshire Terriers, an English Mastiff, and a Yorkie-Chihuahua cross. After a rocky start, all four dogs now share their home in peace. Here, Peggy and Bill share the secrets of their success.

"T-Rex, our six-year-old Yorkie male, was the first to join our household, followed by Sir Henry Higgins, our nine-year-old English Mastiff.

"When a new dog comes to our family, we introduce the dogs in our front yard because it is neutral territory. We take in one dog at a time – on their leashes – just in case of problems.

"Rex and Higgins' first meeting was not a great success, as Rex attempted to attack Higgins before even sniffing him. Fortunately, the dogs were on leashes, so it was easy to pull them apart.

"After correcting Rex and calming both dogs, we tried again. We let the dogs approach each other again, and Higgins stood his ground. After a little growling on Rex's part, the dogs tentatively accepted each other and now they get on very well.

PENNY FOR THEM

"Next to join our family was Penny, a one-year-old female Yorkie-Chihuahua cross, followed by Bitzy, our four-year-old Yorkshire Terrier female. Both the girls barked at Higgins when they arrived, but they settled down very quickly.

"All four dogs are now the best of friends. Rex, Penny, and Bitz will clean Higgins' face, share his water bowl, and lie down next to him. However, they will not share treats and toys – they take them out of his mouth and run off with them! Higgins puts up with it all good-naturedly. The Yorkies are fed separately from Higgins, so that he doesn't get them mixed up with his food!

"Sleeping arrangements are quite amusing in our house. The three small dogs usually sleep on the bed, while Higgins sleeps on the floor, alongside. Higgins tends to get used as a step stool when the Yorkies want to get on and off the bed! He doesn't seem to mind.

"Generally, we have found that Yorkies mix very well with other breeds of dog. A well-raised dog has an even, self-confident temperament, and, provided both dogs have this temperament, a Yorkie will get along with a dog of any breed. However, because Yorkies are so small, you have to be careful if you are thinking of introducing a breed with a high prey drive.

TINY TERRORS

"We foster Yorkshire Terriers, and we have found, quite frequently, that they can be overly aggressive to our Mastiff. Many Yorkies will try to be the dominant member in a household and they must not be allowed to push the other dog too far. Even though Higgins is a very tolerant dog, most dogs will try to defend themselves if they think they are going to get hurt. I keep all my dogs separated until I am sure they understand that aggressive behavior will not be tolerated under any circumstances.

"It is important that all the dogs understand who is in charge of the household. If you establish yourself as the boss, and you make it clear that bad behavior will not be tolerated, you should not have any problems sharing your home with two breeds as diverse as a Yorkshire Terrier and an English Mastiff; you should just have a lot of fun!"

RAINING CATS AND DOGS

Becky Warren, from Indianapolis, Indiana, owns 12 cats and two Yorkies, all of whom share the house in relative harmony.

"My mother and I bred Yorkies for about 20 years, and I retired my last pair in 1999. Now, I have two Yorkies sharing my house – Oh Susie Que (Susie) and Diligent C. Charles Barkley (Barkley). I've been breeding cats since 1985, and I have my own small cattery – Purwaky. At the moment, I have about 12 purebred cats. Some are pets that live in the house with me and share my bed, while others are breeding stock. All are loved and cherished.

Susie and Goldie have learned to live in harmony.

"I've never had any problems letting my Yorkies mix with my cats. I let the dogs and the cats introduce themselves. To begin with, the Yorkies followed the cats around the house, wanting to play. The dogs also wanted to be mothers to the small kittens, trying to lick them and clean them.

"My Yorkies love my cats and they tolerate each other very well. Occasionally, Barkley gets a bit jealous. He tries to nudge the cats out of the way, so that he can have all the attention, but he still plays with the cats, and, most of the time, he adores them. I remember one occasion when one of my breeding Persians went into heat. Barkley tried to mate her. She was bigger than Barkley and boxed him around the ears to let him know she wasn't interested, but his feelings weren't really hurt.

"Anyone thinking of sharing their home with a Yorkie and a cat, doesn't have anything to worry about. All my pets get along famously, and I really enjoy spending time with them and watching them play together. They are such playful and affectionate animals."

- Put your puppy in his crate or in a traveling box, and allow your cat to come up and investigate. This will give her the chance to sniff your puppy without being jumped on.
- Now hold the puppy on your lap, and allow the cat to come up and sniff. Reward your puppy by giving him a treat.
- Repeat this on a number of occasions until both the cat and the puppy are familiar with each other. Work on distracting your puppy with a treat or a toy if he becomes too focused on the cat.

- Next, allow your puppy on the floor, and be ready to distract his attention with a treat if he tries to chase the cat. It is also important to ensure that the cat has access to a chair or a shelf so she has an upward escape route.
- Supervise all interactions for the first few weeks so that your pup never has the opportunity to run after the cat. If he never starts chasing, he will not see it as a natural reaction every time he sees the cat.

Be patient. It takes a while to work out canine/feline relations, but it is well worth working on this aspect of socializing your puppy, so that he never has the chance to get into bad habits. In time, the pair will learn to live in harmony – they may even become good friends!

CRATE-TRAINING

If you are planning to use a crate, you should start by introducing your pup to the crate, and then get him used to staying in it.

- Make the crate look as inviting as possible. Line it with cozy bedding, and place a couple of toys inside. Some owners drape a blanket over the crate, so that it is even more den-like.
- Place your puppy inside the crate. Stroke him and give him a treat, as you kneel alongside the crate, keeping the door open.
- Progress to closing the door for a few minutes, while you stay beside the crate. Talk to your puppy and reassure him so that he does not feel worried or frightened.

- The next stage is to put your puppy in the crate and move away from it. Stay in the same room, and give the puppy a chance to adjust. Obviously, it helps if you choose a time when the puppy is tired and needs to sleep.
- Do not be in too much of a hurry to release your puppy if he starts to cry. It is important that he learns that the crate is his safe haven where he can rest undisturbed.
- It may help if you feed your puppy in his crate, at least to begin with, as this will help to build up a good, positive association.

In no time, your puppy will accept his crate and will be happy to spend time in there. It is essential to obey the following rules:

- Never put your puppy in his crate for long periods (except overnight). An adult dog should never be left for more than four hours, and a young puppy should not be left for this length of time to begin with.

Spend some time reassuring your puppy, and he will soon learn to settle down in his crate.

- Never use the crate as a means of punishment. Your Yorkie should value his crate; he should not feel he is being put in there to be deprived of human company.

HOUSE-TRAINING

This important aspect of your puppy's training should start from the moment he arrives in his new home.

- Take your puppy to the area in the yard that you have allocated for toilet-training. When he relieves himself, give lots of praise.
- It is helpful if you introduce a verbal command, such as "Be clean"; your puppy will associate the command with the action.
- After your puppy has "performed," do not go straight back into the house. Stay in the yard and have a short game. If you rush straight in, your puppy may delay relieving himself simply to prolong the time he spends in the yard.

A small puppy needs to be taken outside frequently. For example:
- First thing in the morning.
- After mealtimes.
- After play sessions.
- At least every two hours during the day.
- Last thing at night.

If you see the telltale signs of your puppy circling and sniffing, you will know he needs to be taken out. It is important to accompany your puppy on every occasion – even if it is raining!

Your puppy needs to be given the command to relieve himself, and then rewarded for the

Take your puppy to the yard at regular intervals, making sure you always go to the same spot.

correct response. In this way, he will learn what is required, and accidents will be kept to a minimum.

Nighttime training

It is impossible for a tiny Yorkie puppy to go through the night without needing to relieve himself. If you are using a dog bed, put some newspaper on the floor, a short distance away from the bed. A puppy will avoid soiling his bed at all costs, so he will, hopefully, use the newspaper instead. Some breeders "paper-train" the litter before they leave for their new homes, so your puppy may have a head start.

If you are using a crate, you can capitalize on your puppy's natural instinct to be clean. Place the bedding at the back of the crate, and line the front half with newspaper. Your puppy will opt to use the paper rather than soiling his bedding. You will probably find that a crate-trained puppy quickly learns to go through the night.

When accidents happen

It is inevitable that your puppy will make the odd "mistake" in the house. Do not scold him, or worse still, rub his nose in it. Nine times out of ten, it will be your fault for forgetting to take your puppy out, or for missing the signs that should tell you he needs to relieve himself. In most cases, you will not discover the accident until some time afterward, so your puppy will have no idea why he is being punished.

If you catch your puppy red-handed, you can take action. Say "*No*" in a deep, firm voice, pick up your puppy, and take him outside. Give the command "*Be clean,*" wait until he has relieved himself, and then give lots of praise.

If your puppy has an accident in the house, make sure you clean it up thoroughly, using a deodorizer. If a puppy can smell the spot, he may be tempted to relieve himself in the same place on subsequent occasions.

Work hard at house-training for the first few weeks, and your puppy will soon get the message. However, do not become complacent and think you have cracked house-training in record time. You will need to do the thinking for your puppy for several months, remembering to take him out at regular intervals. In this way, his mistakes will be few and far between, and, in time, he will ask you when he needs to be taken out.

MEALTIMES

When your puppy arrives home, he will probably require four meals a day. The breeder will provide you with a timetable, and will state how much food to give at each meal. In most cases,

you will be given a supply of food to last for the first couple of days. This is to ensure that the puppy does not have to cope with a change of diet on top of the trauma of moving. A tiny puppy is very prone to digestive upset in these circumstances, and a change of diet will inevitably aggravate the situation.

For the first couple of meals, your puppy may be reluctant to eat. This is because he is preoccupied with his new surroundings, and does not feel relaxed enough to eat. He will also miss the rivalry of feeding with his littermates and having to compete for his food. If this happens, do not worry. Give your puppy ten minutes to eat what is in his bowl, and then discard any leftovers. Give him fresh food when the next meal is due. You will probably find that your puppy's appetite picks up within a couple of days, and he will be wolfing down his rations.

If your puppy continues to show a lack of interest, you can try adding a little grated cheese or gravy to the feed to make it more appetizing. However, if you are worried about

It is best to stick to the diet your puppy is used to.

your puppy's appetite, or if he has diarrhea, you should consult your veterinarian.

CHOOSING A DIET

There is a wide range of different diets available, but, in most cases, you would be well advised to continue with the diet recommended by your puppy's breeder. The breeder will have considerable experience in feeding Yorkshire Terriers, and will know which diet is most appropriate. Complete diets are most commonly fed, as they are easy to feed, and you can be confident that your puppy is getting a balanced diet, which fulfills all the needs of a growing puppy. The problem with feeding a complete diet is that some puppies find them rather plain and unappetizing. The way to tackle this is to add a little cooked chicken or some grated cheese to the meal, which will tempt your puppy's appetite.

If you decide to change the diet because of problems with supply, or because your puppy is not thriving on it, you should make the changeover gradually to avoid a stomach upset. Add a little of the new food at each meal, gradually reducing the original diet. Continue with this over a period of three to four days until you have made a complete transition.

In most cases, the breeder will recommend that you cut down to three meals a day by the time the puppy is around 16 weeks of age. However, it is wise to be guided by your puppy. If he is eating all his food with relish, he needs to stay on four meals for a little longer. In most cases, a puppy will start to leave some of his food (often the lunchtime meal), which will tell you

that he is ready to reduce to three meals a day. By the time your puppy is six months of age, he should be fed twice a day – once in the morning and once in the evening – and you should continue with this routine into adulthood.

For information on feeding adult Yorkies, see page 69.

THE FIRST NIGHT

At the end of the first day in his new home, your puppy will be exhausted. However, he will still find the energy to put up a struggle when the time comes to put him to bed. Looking at it from the puppy's point of view, this is hardly surprising. He has spent the day getting used to his new family; now, he is being deserted, and is expected to settle down without the comforting presence of his littermates.

It is important to decide what policy you are going to adopt in relation to sleeping arrangements. If you are happy to let your dog sleep in your bedroom, or even on your bed, that is fine. It is a matter of personal choice – and your puppy will be happy to cooperate. However, if you want your puppy to go to his own bed, or settle in his crate, you must be firm. If you give into protests, you will find that he soon gets the upper hand, and will continue crying until you come to "rescue" him.

In fact, it is not difficult to settle a puppy at night if you adopt the following routine:

- Take your puppy out to relieve himself.
- Put the puppy in his crate, or in his dog bed. You can give him a treat, and spend a couple

Your puppy is used to the company of his littermates, so he will feel lonely to begin with.

The first night will be the worst, but if you leave your puppy undisturbed, he will learn that there is nothing to fear about being left alone at night. He will be reunited with his family in the morning, and he will soon accept the nighttime routine without protest.

HOUSE RULES

When you take on a puppy, you need to divide his training into two areas. You will need to teach basic obedience exercises (see Chapter Four), but you will also need to educate your pup to live in the house as a member of the family.

To achieve this, your puppy needs to understand what constitutes acceptable behavior. Some owners are quite happy if the dog sleeps on the furniture and begs

of minutes stroking him and reassuring him before leaving the room.

- Some owners leave a ticking clock in the room, or leave the radio on with the volume turned low, as this can be a comfort.
- Inevitably your puppy will cry, but if you ignore him, he will have no option but to settle down. He will be very tired, and eventually he will go to sleep.

Obviously, it is much easier if the puppy is in a crate, as he cannot get into any mischief. If your puppy is not confined, you must make a thorough check of the room to be sure he cannot get into trouble.

Make sure you are always consistent with your training.

at the table; other people prefer to keep a closer check on their dog's behavior. It is important to decide what rules your dog should obey, and then stick to them. Your Yorkie will be quite happy if he is told that he must stay in his dog bed. However, he will become very confused if he is usually allowed to go on the furniture, and then he is told off if he tries to get on the sofa when he has muddy paws.

Be consistent in your training, and make sure all members of the family stick to the same rules. The Yorkie is a very quick learner, and your puppy will soon become a model member of the family.

GROOMING

When you look at a Yorkie puppy, it is hard to believe that his coat will become his crowning glory. The average puppy has an endearing, tousled appearance, and looks more like a miniature crossbreed than a purebred Yorkshire Terrier.

However, it is essential that you do not delay grooming until the adult coat comes through. The long coat of the Yorkshire Terrier requires a huge amount of care – even if you are not planning to show your dog – and your puppy must learn to accept grooming as a routine part of his daily life. In most cases, the breeder will have started this work, getting each puppy used to being handled and to being groomed with a brush and a comb. It is your job to carry on with this, so that your Yorkie is totally at ease with the concept of being groomed, in preparation for the time when he will need extensive work.

The first stage is to get your puppy used to being handled all over. This is important when it comes to grooming, but it is also important if your dog has to be examined by the veterinarian. You will probably find it easier if you get your Yorkie used to standing on a table. This will mean that grooming is not a backbreaking business. You can buy a specially built grooming table, or you can use a picnic table, first placing a rubber mat on the surface so that your puppy cannot slip.

Handling

- Start by stroking your puppy and reassuring him. You can give him a treat to encourage him to stay on the table.
- Examine your puppy's ears, looking into each one to ensure that it is clean and smells fresh.
- Check both eyes, and clean away debris.
- Open your puppy's mouth and check his teeth. It is a good idea to have an extra treat to give your puppy after you have looked at his teeth. Some puppies can be sensitive in this area, particularly when teething (see page 126), so it is helpful if you give a treat as an instant reward. This will encourage your puppy to be cooperative on future occasions.
- Pick up each paw in turn, and check the nails and the pads.
- Turn your puppy onto his back, and tickle his tummy. Most puppies enjoy this, and it encourages all-over handling.
- Stroke your puppy from head to tail, and hold onto his tail for a few seconds. Give lots of praise and reassurance.

HANDLING

▲ *Examine your puppy's ears.*

▲ *Check the teeth.*

▲ *Pick up each paw in turn.*

Use a soft bristle ▶
brush, and
gently brush the
coat.

◀ *Then work*
through the coat
with a comb.

The nails can be
trimmed using ▶
scissors or
nail clippers.

Coat care

The next stage is to accustom your puppy to being groomed. If he is used to being handled, this should pose few problems. Remember to keep a supply of treats handy, and reward your puppy when he is cooperating. Talk to your puppy, encouraging him to enjoy the quality time he is spending with you. In time, most Yorkies actively enjoy grooming sessions; they find it very relaxing, and they thrive on the one-to-one attention.

• Start by using a soft, bristle brush, and gently brush through your puppy's coat. If your puppy struggles, keep the session short, and reward him if he sits quietly for just a few strokes of the brush. In the initial stages, the aim is for your puppy to accept the attention, albeit fleetingly, rather than worry about doing a thorough job.

• Now use a comb, and work your way through the coat.

• In most cases, the breeder will have accustomed the puppies to this routine, so your puppy should be willing to cooperate.

• Remember to reward good behavior, and do not expect your young Yorkie to stay still for too long.

Nails

The breeder will have trimmed the puppies' nails from an early age to prevent them from scratching their mother while they were feeding. You can trim off the tips of the nails with scissors, or you may prefer to use nail clippers.

Dental care

Your puppy should get used to opening his mouth and having his teeth examined. This is important for a prospective show dog (see Chapter Eight), but it should also be a matter of routine for a pet. Teeth will need to be cleaned on a regular basis in order to prevent problems with tooth decay and gum infection (see page 72).

To start with, open your puppy's mouth for just a few seconds, and then reward him with a treat or a game with a toy. Do not struggle with your puppy, or he will begin to resent your interference. Give lots of praise, and gradually work at building up the amount of time your puppy will keep his mouth open.

When your puppy first arrives in his new home, he will still have his milk teeth. At around four months, he will shed these teeth, and they will be replaced by permanent, adult teeth. You will need to check your puppy's mouth when he is teething to ensure that the adult teeth are coming through correctly. At this stage, his gums may be quite sore, so be gentle with your handling. The puppy may also have a strong desire to chew while his new teeth are erupting, so make sure you provide dental chews, as well as some suitable toys.

VISITING THE VETERINARIAN

When your puppy has had a few days to settle in, take him to your veterinarian for a checkup. Make sure this trip is as untraumatic as possible, as you want your puppy to look on the veterinarian as a friend rather than as his worst enemy.

Bring some treats, so you can reward your puppy when he is handled by the veterinarian. You may find that the veterinarian has his own supply! At this stage, the veterinarian will give a general examination to be sure your puppy is fit and healthy. If you have a male dog, it is worth asking the veterinarian to check if the puppy has two normally descended testicles.

Take the opportunity to discuss worming procedures with your veterinarian, and then make arrangements for your puppy's vaccination program.

SOCIALIZING YOUR PUPPY

It is now widely recognized that providing a comprehensive program of socialization is essential in rearing a well-balanced dog who will be calm and sensible in all situations.

A young puppy soaks up new experiences like a sponge, and your puppy's aptitude to learn is at its greatest in the first couple of months in his new home. If he is exposed to a wide variety of new experiences, and is taught to react in the correct manner, he will be learning lessons for life.

The breeder will have started socializing the litter, getting them used to household sights and sounds. You must continue this work by familiarizing your puppy with all the household equipment, such as the vacuum cleaner and the washing machine. Your puppy may be a bit tentative to begin with – machines can seem like noisy, frightening monsters to a tiny puppy – but he will soon overcome his nerves if you are on hand to give praise and reassurance. If your puppy appears nervous, make sure he is not too

The importance of socialization is now widely accepted.

close to the machine, and distract his attention with a treat or a game. Next time, follow the same routine, but position yourself a bit closer to the machine. Proceed in small stages, and your puppy will soon forget he was ever frightened.

Once your puppy is settled in his new home, you can invite visitors to meet the new arrival. This will give him the opportunity to make friends with strangers, getting him used to different voices, and the different way people dress. We may think nothing of a friend arriving wearing a hat or a pair of dark glasses, but these are all new experiences for a youngster.

CAR TRAVEL

A Yorkie loves to be involved in family activities, and a trip out in the car provides an interesting

Your Yorkie will be far safer if he travels in a carrier.

change in routine. However, you will need to train your puppy so that he learns to settle down in the car. If you wait until your Yorkie is grown up before trying this, he will make a terrible fuss, and may well become a bad traveler for the rest of his life.

The best plan is to use a carrier in the car, so that your Yorkie is 100 percent safe and secure. To begin with, get your Yorkie used to going in his carrier. This is done in exactly the same way as crate-training (see page 35). Reward your puppy every time he goes in his carrier, as this will act as an incentive.

To begin with, take your Yorkie for short trips in the car. Some people find that playing the car radio has a soothing effect. At any event, it helps to drown out your puppy's protests! Generally, a puppy will settle down quickly and go to sleep – particularly if you have lined the carrier with some cozy bedding.

When your puppy has completed his vaccinations, you can make sure that a car trip ends in something pleasurable, such as a walk in the park, and then your Yorkie will start to look forward to his outings in the car.

If you continue to experience problems with car travel, ask your veterinarian for advice. There are some effective carsickness remedies, and there is also medication available that will help an overexcitable dog calm down.

THE OUTSIDE WORLD

When your puppy has completed his vaccinations, you will be ready to venture into the outside world. This can be daunting for a Yorkie puppy, so do not rush straight into the thick of a busy shopping thoroughfare. Start by going to a quiet place, and maybe sit on a bench with your puppy on your lap. In this way, the puppy can watch the world going by, and you can give him gentle reassurance.

When your puppy is becoming more confident, it is important that you let him stand on his feet. Although a Yorkie is small enough to carry, you do not want your puppy to become so dependent that he thinks he cannot cope on his own. When your puppy is walking reasonably well on the lead (see page 53), take him for short outings to the park, or go to a quiet neighborhood where the traffic is is frightened by something, such as roadwork, or the hiss of airbrakes as a truck passes, do not rush to pick him up. If you appear concerned, your puppy will think there really is something to be frightened of. Give him reassurance, and distract his attention with a treat or a favorite toy, and then encourage him to walk with you. Do not make the mistake of avoiding things your puppy has been worried about. If he is exposed to a situation on a regular basis, and given reassurance, he will soon learn there is nothing to fear.

You can build up your program of socialization stage by stage. Here are some ideas:

- Practice going up and down stairs.
- Visit a shop that has a slippery, tile floor.
- Go to a shopping center.
- Take a trip to see some livestock, e.g. cows, sheep, horses, or poultry.
- Go to a busy street market.

A well-socialized Yorkie will take new experiences in his stride.

not too heavy. Encourage your puppy to walk with you, but if he stops to look at something, do not yank him to follow you. Give him a chance to investigate, and then encourage him to continue on his way. It may help if you have a treat to distract his attention. If your puppy

This is a wonderful period when you can teach your puppy about the outside world, and build up your own relationship with him at the same time. Your puppy will learn to look on you as his leader, and the more time you spend working on your socialization program, the more well adjusted your Yorkie will be in adult life.

CHAPTER FOUR

TRAINING TARGETS

Once your puppy has settled into his new home, and you have established basic house rules, you can start to develop a training program. You may think that a dog that is as small as a Yorkshire Terrier will not need much in the way of training – but that would be making a big mistake.

One of the great pleasures of owning a Yorkie is that you have a dog that you can take everywhere.

However, you need to be confident that you also have a dog that will behave in all situations. Your Yorkie may be small in size, but he is an expert in making his presence felt. That is no bad thing when you have a dog you can be proud of – but if your dog is a nuisance, refusing to do what he is told, you will soon find yourself short of friends.

MEASURING INTELLIGENCE

How do you measure how intelligent a dog is? Most people would point to the Border Collie or the Golden Retriever – both are stars of Competitive Obedience, Agility, and Flyball – as being the canine superbrains. There is no doubt that Collies and Goldens are lightning quick to learn, but behind every successful canine competitor is a handler who has trained the dog to a high degree of excellence.

The Yorkshire Terrier is not the obvious choice for a competition dog, but there is no doubting his intelligence. He is quick-witted, fast moving, and tunes into new training situations with alacrity. On the downside, there is the terrier side to the Yorkie's character. This is a breed that has a mind of his own, and he will not obey unless he sees a good reason to do so. If you want slavelike obedience, choose another breed!

UNDERSTANDING LEADERSHIP

The Yorkshire Terrier does not bear a strong resemblance to a wolf. Thousands of years of specialized breeding and domestication have made huge changes in the way dogs look, but interestingly, not in the way they behave. All dogs are descended from wolves, and they retain a total understanding of what is entailed in living in a pack.

Right from the time they are born, a mother will teach her puppies to respect her. She will give a warning growl if they overstep the mark, and, as the puppies get older, she will be quite rough in her dealings with them. This is the canine way of bringing up puppies to respect their elders.

In the wild, the youngsters have to find their place in their pack. They learn to be submissive to the pack leader, and accept his authority. As they mature, they may move up in status, and a dog with a dominant nature may try to challenge the established leadership.

How does this translate to a domestic situation? Your Yorkie puppy will have received his first lessons in respecting authority from his mother, and the rough-and-tumble between brothers and sisters will also have given him a grounding in canine manners. He will have learned when he can be top puppy, and when it is wiser to give in gracefully.

When your Yorkie puppy arrives home, your task is to continue his education. He needs to learn how to relate to other dogs (see page 31), but more importantly, he needs to find his place in the human pack that he has become a member of.

In the old school of dog training, a lot of emphasis was put on becoming a "pack leader" so that your dog would learn to "submit" to your authority. All too often, harsh handling

Your puppy must learn to understand the concept of leadership.

techniques were used to reinforce the status quo, and a dog obeyed through fear rather than respect. Now, modern methods of training are based on a positive system of praise and reward. This is entirely for the good, and the result is a happy dog who does as he is told because he wants to please, and is working for a reward.

However, it is important that a dog still understands that you are his leader. This does not mean that you should be a stern disciplinarian, barking orders at a poor, defenseless puppy; instead you should show that you are someone who should be respected. You can play with your puppy and have lots of fun together, but you should set the boundaries and correct your puppy if he oversteps them. You provide his food, his creature comforts, and his security, and so he must learn to abide by the rules you have laid down.

If you tune into this way of thinking, you will have a contented dog that understands what is required of him. If you fail to provide leadership, you will end up with an unhappy, difficult dog that is constantly challenging the rules and that lacks a sense of security.

STARTING POINT

Most Yorkie puppies are around ten weeks old when they move to their new homes. You may think that this is far too young to start training, but, in fact, the sooner you start, the better.

A young puppy is tremendously receptive, and although his concentration span is limited, he will be very quick to learn. On the plus side, this means your puppy will be swift to learn basic training exercises, but he will be equally quick to learn bad habits. The wise trainer gets in first, and teaches desirable behavior before the quick-witted Yorkie has made up his own agenda!

The first job is to discover what motivates your puppy. You need to find a reward that he really values, and will work hard to get. In the majority of cases, food is the key. This is an instant, tangible reward, and a Yorkie will be quick to see that if he does what you ask, he will get what he wants. Obviously, you have to bear in mind that you are working with a very small Toy dog, and you cannot heap large quantities of food on him during a training session. If you do, you will soon end up with an obese pet that is too lethargic to do anything for you.

If you decide to use food as a reward, you should deduct the food you use in training sessions from your dog's daily ration. It is also a good idea to try to find a treat that your dog

Most puppies will be motivated by a food reward.

really appreciates. This could be cheese, cooked chicken, or sausage – your Yorkie will soon let you know which is his favorite. If the treat is truly mouthwatering (as far as your Yorkie is concerned), he will pull out all the stops in order to work for it.

When you are preparing for a training session, cut your chosen treats into tiny pieces, so that you have to give only a small amount as a reward. If you prefer, you can use processed cheese, which you can buy from the supermarket. The advantage of this type of treat is that you can literally give your pup a tiny lick from your fingers, rather than giving him anything more substantial. As your dog progresses in training, you will not have to reward for every correct

CLICKER TRAINING

This is a relatively new form of training that is proving highly successful with all types of animals from horses to ferrets – not forgetting dogs! The system was adapted to dogs by Karen Pryor from her work with dolphins.

The clicker is a small box, fitted with a tonguelike clicker, which is operated by pressing with the thumb. It is used to acknowledge correct behavior, which is instantly followed by a reward. The reward is generally a food treat, but it can be a game with a toy, or simply verbal praise and stroking. The dog quickly learns that he must "earn" a click in order to get his reward, and so he will work hard to offer the correct behavior.

The great advantage of the clicker is that it gives a very precise means of saying: "Yes, that is the behavior I want."

The timing of the reward is not important, it is the "click" that tells the dog he has responded correctly.

There are now many training clubs that specialize in clicker training, and you will find that it is an enjoyable and effective way of training your Yorkie.

move he makes. You will be able to give a reward at the end of an exercise, or even on a random basis. This keeps your dog highly motivated, as he has to keep on working, and training sessions never become dull and predictable.

Some Yorkies will not work for food treats. They may enjoy mealtimes, but they are not obsessed by food, and so they do not see the point of working for a tiny morsel. If your puppy is not a foodie, you will have to find a different reward that he is prepared to work for. In most cases, a special training toy will do the trick. Yorkies love playing with toys, and the terrier instinct to get a toy and hang on to it is very strong.

Experiment with a few different toys, and find out what really excites your dog. When you find the right toy – it could be a ball, a squeaky toy, or a soft, furry toy – keep it on one side and only produce it at training sessions. This gives the toy terrific novelty value, and your Yorkie will do his very best for you in order to play

with his toy. In the same way as you reduce food treats as training progresses, you can limit access to the toy, and then have a really big play session when your Yorkie goes the extra mile.

TRAINING EXERCISES

In the following exercises, the clicker is used as a means of training. If you do not wish to use a clicker, do exactly as prescribed, without the clicker, making sure you give lavish praise and reward.

Remember, a puppy has a very short attention span, so training sessions should be kept short and enjoyable. Aim for producing some good-quality work in a five-minute session, and then end with a game. In this way, your Yorkie will look forward to his training, and he will try his best for you.

Sit

This is the simplest exercise to teach, and it is rewarding for both you and your puppy to

Use a treat to lure your puppy into the Sit.

To train the Down, *close your hand over a treat and lower it to the floor.*

achieve fairly instant success. In the show world, owners often bypass this exercise, as the last thing you want is a dog that sits in the show ring. However, if your dog learns to respond to "*Sit*" and "*Stand*" as separate commands, it should not pose a problem.

- Prepare some food treats, and hold one in your hand just above your puppy's head.
- Your puppy will look up at the treat, and, in his effort to reach it, he will lower his hindquarters. The moment he does this, click and reward.
- Repeat the exercise, and wait until your puppy has gone into the *sit* before giving a click and a reward.
- Repeat the exercise several times a day until your puppy is instantly going into the *sit* when you hold the treat above his head.
- You can also repeat the exercise at mealtimes, holding the food bowl just above your puppy's head.
- When you are confident that your puppy fully

understands the exercise, introduce the verbal command "*Sit*" as your puppy goes into position. In no time, he will associate the command with the action, so that he will respond to your voice rather than being lured into position.

Once your puppy is fully proficient, reward on a random basis. You can still give verbal praise, but a treat should not be given on every occasion. The *sit* is the starting point of many exercises, and, as your Yorkie progresses in his training, he will learn that he has to work a bit harder to get a reward.

Down

This is a progression from the *sit*, and should be taught once your puppy has mastered the former exercise.

- Prepare some treats, and hold one piece in your hand. Make sure your puppy knows you have a treat, and then close your fist.

- Put your puppy in the *sit*, and hold the treat just below his nose. As he starts to sniff the treat, gradually lower it toward the ground.

- In an attempt to get at the treat, your puppy will follow the treat. As he starts to lower his forequarters, click and reward.

- Next time, wait a little longer before clicking and giving the reward, so that your puppy is closer to the *down* position. If necessary, apply gentle pressure to his hindquarters to encourage him to go into position.

- Repeat this exercise several times during the day, and your puppy will learn that he must go into the *down* before getting his reward.

- When your puppy is responding correctly each and every time, introduce the verbal command.

The *down* exercise is relatively easy to teach, and it is one of the most useful of all exercises. If you work at getting an instant response to the command "*Down*," it can even prove to be a lifesaver in an emergency situation.

Stand

This is an important exercise if you plan to show your Yorkie, as he will need to stand in a show pose. For the pet owner, it is valuable when you want to groom your dog, or if he needs to be examined by the veterinarian.

- Start with your puppy in the *sit*, and show him you have a treat in your hand.

- Hold the treat by his nose, and gradually

Hold the treat out from the puppy to maintain the stand.

withdraw your hand. Your puppy will get to his feet to follow the treat. Click and reward.

- Next time, make sure your puppy stands still for a few seconds before clicking and giving the reward.

- It may help if you gently stroke your puppy while he is standing; this will encourage him to stay in position.

- Repeat the exercise over a number of training sessions. At this stage, it is better to work on the *stand* exercise in isolation, so your Yorkie does not get confused with the other stationary exercises.

- When your puppy is going into the *stand* and staying in position, introduce the verbal command "*Stand*." It helps if you draw out the word – "*St-and*," so that your puppy does not confuse it with the *sit* command.

Lead-training

It will take numerous training sessions before your puppy is happy to walk on a loose lead, but the sooner you start, the better. If you reach a reasonable level of proficiency while your puppy is waiting for his inoculations to be completed, you will be ready to take him into the outside world on a lead as soon as he is fully protected.

Before you can start lead-training, your puppy will have to get used to wearing a collar. As discussed earlier, the collar should be soft and lightweight, so that your puppy has a minimal feeling of restraint.

- Fasten the collar around your puppy's neck, making sure you can fit two fingers between his neck and the collar.
- To begin with, your puppy will probably scratch at the collar, and try to remove it. Talk to him calmly, and reward him with a treat. It helps if you can distract his attention by playing a game with his favorite toy.
- Leave the collar on for a few minutes, and then take it off. Next time, you can leave the collar on for a little longer so that he starts getting used to it.
- You can try putting the collar on and then giving your puppy a meal. Few puppies will worry about a collar if they have food in front of them!
- When your puppy ignores his collar, you can introduce the lead. To begin with, attach the lead and allow it to trail, making sure it does not get caught.

- Next, pick up the lead and follow your puppy wherever he chooses to go. Click and reward when your puppy is walking happily on the lead, without showing any resistance.
- The next stage is the hardest. You must now encourage your puppy to follow you rather than the other way around. You will find it easier if you use a treat or a toy to tempt your Yorkie to follow you. As soon as you get a few paces of good heelwork, i.e., your puppy walking alongside you on a loose lead, click and reward.
- This exercise needs to be repeated at every training session, gradually building up the amount of time your puppy will walk on the lead. When you are confident that your puppy understands what is required, introduce the command "*Heel*" or "*Close*."

Be patient with this exercise. It is probably the single most important lesson your Yorkie has to learn, so it is worth taking the trouble to get it right.

- If your puppy lags behind, stop, and encourage him to come up to you by using a treat or a toy. Do not click and reward until you have completed a few paces of good heelwork.
- If your puppy pulls ahead, stop, and call him back to your side, again using a treat or a toy. Do not click and reward until you have set off and completed a few paces of good heelwork.
- As training progresses, you can start off with your Yorkie sitting on your left side, and then

Above: Use a toy or treat to encourage the puppy to follow you.

set off, with your Yorkie walking on your left side. Gradually introduce some turns and some changes of pace, so that your Yorkie learns to stay in position next to you.

The biggest mistake that most handlers make with heelwork is getting the timing wrong. The command *"Heel"* is often incorrectly used when the dog is surging ahead in an attempt to get him back into the correct position, or when the dog is praised for coming back and standing by his handler, rather than when he is walking to heel. It is not surprising that the dog becomes confused and fails to understand what is required.

Think before you act, and work at giving your puppy a clear picture of what you want. Try to keep these sessions short, and break them up with play and reward so that your pup does not start to dread lead-training.

Stay

It is best to leave this exercise until your puppy is happy to work on a lead.

- Start with your puppy on-lead, sitting at your left side. Step one pace to the side, giving a hand signal for your puppy to stay in position. This is usually a hand held out, with the palm facing your pup.
- Step back to your puppy's side, wait a second, and then click and reward.
- Repeat this exercise, stepping two paces away, and then pausing for slightly longer before you click and reward.
- Now put your puppy in the *sit*, and stand in front of him. Take two steps back, wait, and then return to the front of your puppy. Click and reward.
- Repeat the exercise, this time standing next to your puppy, and stepping back a couple of paces. The aim is for your pup to stay in position, regardless of where you are standing.
- Over a number of training sessions, gradually increase the time your pup stays in position before you click and reward. When you are confident that he understands the exercise, introduce the verbal command *"Stay."* It is probably a good idea to continue to back this

You can graduate to working on the stay *off-lead.*

up with a hand signal until your puppy is 100 percent confident.

For this exercise, it is best to keep your praise fairly low-key, so your puppy does not get too excited and break position as you come back to his side. Some handlers find it helpful to use a release word, such as "*Okay,*" so that the dog understands when the exercise has been completed.

Recall

When your puppy first arrives home, you will be delighted with his response to the command "*Come.*" A puppy has an instinctive desire to follow, and you can work on this by calling his name and using the command "*Come*" in all situations. In no time, you will find yourself tripping over your little Yorkie as he tries to keep close to you.

- Build on this behavior by calling your pup to "*Come*" at mealtimes, and then rewarding him with his food bowl.
- When your puppy becomes more confident, you can try calling him when he is in another room. Make sure you click and reward when your puppy comes up to you.
- Recruit a helper to hold onto your puppy, and then release him when you give the command "*Come.*" You can turn this into a game by taking turns calling the puppy. Make sure both handlers have a reward, and limit the game so your puppy doesn't become overtired.

Most puppies are very enthusiastic about this lesson at home, but they lose interest when you move into the yard where there are lots of interesting distractions. Yorkies are particularly guilty of this; they are so busy and interested in everything that is going on, it can be a hard job to focus their attention.

- Recruit a helper to hold onto your Yorkie, and then give the command "*Come.*" Make sure you sound really excited. If necessary, jump up and down, or throw a toy in the air. The aim is to make yourself irresistible so that your Yorkie really wants to come to you. As soon as your puppy responds correctly, click and reward.
- Work on this exercise over a number of training sessions until your Yorkie is responding instantly and enthusiastically. If your puppy hesitates, or is slow to come to you, turn and run a couple of steps in the opposite direction. This will usually stimulate your puppy to run after you. As soon as he responds correctly, click, and give lots of praise and a reward. Coming to you must always mean fun – your puppy should never be reprimanded for a slow response if he comes to you eventually.

In time, you will be able to build up a really enthusiastic response to the come command.

- When your puppy is responding consistently to the *come* command in the yard, you can try a recall in the park. Obviously, your puppy must have completed his vaccinations, and you should choose a place that does not have too many distractions.
- For the first few recalls, use a training line, approximately 9–12 feet (2.7–3.6 meters) in length, and secure one end of it to your Yorkie's collar. Recruit a helper to hold onto your Yorkie, and then call him in while you are a short distance away. The training line does not need to be held; it is simply a safeguard so that you have something to grab if your Yorkie attempts to run off.
- When your Yorkie responds to the *come* command, click and give lots of praise so that your dog is in no doubt that he has done the right thing. Do not be in too much of a rush to take off the training line. It is much better to build up this exercise gradually and develop a strong response, rather than allowing your

GOLDEN RULES FOR RECALL

- Do not attempt a recall off-lead unless you have worked on the exercise at home and you are confident that your Yorkie understands what is required.
- If you allow your Yorkie off-lead, choose a safe place that is as far away from traffic as possible.
- Always reward your Yorkie when he comes to you – no matter how long he takes!
- If you are not confident about your Yorkie's recall, do not take the risk of letting him go off the lead. You can exercise your Yorkie on an extending lead so that he has the opportunity to explore – but you stay in control.

Yorkie to make mistakes and then to get into the habit of ignoring your command to come.

• As training progresses, you can work on a formal recall incorporating a *sit, wait, come,* and then a *sit* as your Yorkie comes in to you. It sounds ambitious when you are starting off, but the intelligent Yorkie is more than capable of learning what is required.

Retrieve

This is not an essential exercise, but your Yorkie will enjoy the stimulation of learning something new, and it provides the means of a ready game.

The Yorkie loves to retrieve – but he can be reluctant to give up his toy.

• Start off by finding a retrieve article that your puppy really likes. This could be a ball or a toy – it does not matter what it is, as long as your Yorkie values it.

• Start off by playing with the toy so that your puppy becomes focused on it. Then, throw the toy a short distance away. As soon as your puppy moves to get it, click and reward.

• Work on this, gradually delaying the click and the reward until your puppy picks up the toy.

• When your puppy is running out and picking up the toy consistently, you can introduce the verbal command "*Hold*" as your puppy picks up the toy.

• The next stage is to get your puppy to bring the toy back to you. If you are lucky, he may bring it back to you on the command "*Come,*" but he will probably think it is more fun to run off with his trophy.

• Prepare some treats, and make sure your puppy knows you have some in your hand.

When he runs out and picks up the toy, call him, and click and reward for any move back in your direction.

• Work on this stage, and soon your puppy will learn that he will not earn his click and his reward unless he brings the toy back to you.

• Some Yorkies are very anxious to hang onto the retrieve toy. In this case, it may help if you have another toy, so that you can do an exchange when your puppy comes to you.

This is quite a complicated exercise, so take your time and work through the stages gradually. Above all, make sure that training sessions are fun so that your Yorkie looks forward to the time he is spending with you.

FUN TRICKS

The purpose of training is to control your dog so that he is a civilized and well-behaved companion. But there is another, equally important reason. Training provides mental stimulation for your dog, and in a breed that is as lively and intelligent as a Yorkie, this is essential. If your dog becomes bored, his mind will quickly turn to mischief.

Training is a way of spending quality time interacting with your Yorkie. He will benefit from having his mind exercised, he will thrive on the attention he is being given, and your relationship will improve as you work through stages in training, giving praise, and rewarding his efforts.

Once your Yorkie has mastered the basic exercises, do not give up on him. Introduce some fun tricks, such as giving his paw, sitting up and begging, or rolling over on command. These tricks are easy to teach with the aid of a clicker. The key is to break down each trick into modules, and click and reward at each stage before moving on to the next. Your Yorkie will have great fun learning new tricks, and he will love performing in front of an audience.

TRAINING CLASSES

When your Yorkie is fully vaccinated, it is a good idea to join a training club, but before you sign up, you should attend a class without your pup and check out the following:

- Do the instructors use positive training methods, relying on praise and reward rather than harsh, corrective training? If you see any signs of pulling, yanking, or shouting at dogs, you would be advised to look elsewhere.
- Do the instructors use clicker training? This is

Your Yorkie will love to perform some fun tricks.

not essential, but you and your Yorkie can benefit from experienced trainers who are well versed in this method of training.

- Are the classes well run? Ideally, dogs of similar ability should be trained together, with the opportunity to progress into the higher classes. This may not be possible if the club has only a small membership, but you should be confident that the instructor can cater to a range of abilities.
- Do the instructors have experience training Toy dogs – ideally Yorkshire Terriers? It is important that an instructor understands how your dog's mind works, and has realistic expectations of what he can achieve.

If you are happy with what you see, you can start taking your Yorkie to classes. Hopefully, you will both benefit from these outings, gaining from the advice offered, and enjoying the company of dogs and owners alike.

If you plan to show your dog, or you are interested in getting involved in one of the canine sports, you will need to find a special club (See Chapter Seven: The Versatile Yorkie).

CHAPTER FIVE

THE ADOLESCENT YORKIE

O nce you have passed out of the puppy stage, you might think that it would all be plain sailing – but there is a small matter of adolescence to go through. This is when the hormones kick in, and, understandably, your Yorkie may go through some behavioral changes before he emerges as a mature adult. Do not despair if you seem to take one pace forward and two paces back at this time. If you stay calm and adopt a positive attitude, you will be able to guide your dog through this difficult phase with the minimum of upset.

WHAT IS GOING ON?

Just as human teenagers are notoriously difficult, adolescent animals can be equally trying. It is the time when the body becomes sexually mature, the hormones start to pump around the body, and the adolescent starts to question the status quo. A puppy may be naughty and misbehave, but, in the hands of a sensible owner, he is eager to please and is ready to accept authority. An adolescent dog – male and female alike – suddenly questions its subordinate role in the family. Instead of living with a lively youngster that may be a bit boisterous but is basically on your side, you are confronted with a truculent or stubborn individual that constantly asks the question, "Why should I?"

Bitches generally hit adolescence from six months on. They may have their first season as young as five months, or as late as 22 months, but the average Yorkie bitch will have her first season at around eight months of age. Yorkie males are late to mature. Most will exhibit adolescent behavior from around 12 months, and will not be fully mature until 18 months of age.

HOW DO I COPE?

Adolescent behavior sounds like a nightmare, but it is mercifully short-lived – particularly if you know how to handle the teenage tantrums. Jenny Langhoon has bred Yorkies for 28 years, and has shown them with considerable success under her Yorlang affix for the last 18 years. She has seen numerous Yorkies pass through their adolescence – and she is still here to tell the tale!

"My advice is to take a deep breath, and then give you and your dog a break," she said. "If you become confrontational, you will only make things worse. For example, if a youngster suddenly decides he is not going to move in the show ring, there is no point making a big issue of it and insisting that he will do as you ask. All you are doing is introducing the dominant factor and asking to be challenged. This does not work with Yorkies.

"In the show ring, I would simply stop showing a Yorkie that has decided to put up a fight, or that is refusing to listen to instructions. Forget all about your ambitions with that dog for a few months, and leave him at home. This will prevent bad behavior from becoming a habit. When you try again, your Yorkie will have forgotten all about his previous misdemeanors.

"In a home situation, I would give the same advice, but it has to be channelled in a slightly different way. I find the best thing to do is to withdraw your attention. If a dog is misbehaving, I would correct him with a firm "*No,*" and then I would ignore him by not speaking to him and avoiding eye contact. A Yorkie thrives on attention; if this is withdrawn, he will be at a loss.

"The mistake many owners make is to go on talking to a dog that has misbehaved, explaining to him what he has done wrong and why they are upset. As far as the dog is concerned, he is getting attention, and that is good enough for him. In his own mind, his bad behavior has brought about a good result, so why not repeat it in the future?

"I have found that tone of voice is the most effective way of disciplining a Yorkie. If you teach a puppy right from the beginning that "*No,*" spoken in a deep, gruff voice, means the behavior must end, he will understand what is required. If this is coupled with withdrawing your attention, the dog will know there is no point in challenging you any further. He has tested the boundaries, and you have shown him exactly where he stands.

"In all my time in Yorkies, I have come across very few bad dogs, but many bad owners. If we teach our dogs how to behave, and we give them clear guidelines so that they understand what is expected of them, there is no need for conflict."

Ch. Yorlang Amazing Grace (left) and Ch. Yorlang Sweet. Be patient with your adolescent Yorkie, and you will be rewarded with an adult that is a pleasure to live with.

ADOLESCENT BEHAVIOR

Obviously, adolescent dogs express their feelings in a variety of ways, and there will be differences between males and females. Typically, a female Yorkie will have a great surge of energy, and will decide to take on the world at her own frenetic pace. In the show ring, she may fly up and down the ring, while the pet Yorkie may have crazy bouts of play, roaring around the house or the yard. At other times, the adolescent female Yorkie may feel withdrawn and off-color, and everything will be too much trouble for her.

The male can be self-willed and unco-operative as he hits adolescence. He will often go from being a "mommy's boy," desperate to please his owner, to being stubborn and determined to do what he pleases. He is pushing back the boundaries and seeing how far he can go.

TROUBLESHOOTING

There are a few difficulties that can crop up in adolescence, which can become problems for life unless they are handled correctly. Advice is given on some of the more common problems that occur, but if you feel you are not making any progress, or your dog has a different type of problem, do not delay in seeking the help of a qualified animal behaviorist.

Barking

Toy breeds have a reputation for being "yappy" dogs, but, in fact, this slur on their character is largely undeserved. There is no doubt that a

Yorkies are always on the alert, and this can lead to excessive barking.

Yorkie likes to make his presence known. He may be small, but he has a great sense of his own importance and is eager to be the focus of attention. However, there is no reason why this aspect of a Yorkie's character should be expressed by barking.

There is nothing wrong with giving a warning bark if visitors are calling, or to giving an occasional bark of excitement during a game. But the Yorkie that yaps continuously when you have visitors, or when you are attempting to train him or play with him, is a menace.

There are two ways to tackle this problem. First, be quick to correct your Yorkie when he barks inappropriately. You can use a command such as *"Quiet,"* and be ready with a reward when your Yorkie stops barking. In time, he will learn that "*Quiet*" means that if he stops barking, he gets a treat. If your Yorkie continues to bark, withdraw your attention, so he is not rewarded by you making a fuss over him. If necessary, leave the room, and only return when your Yorkie is quiet. In this way, he will learn that barking is counterproductive, and being quiet results in a reward.

The second method of tackling inappropriate barking is to teach your Yorkie to bark! When he barks, give the command "*Speak,*" and reward him. Then, introduce a command for him to stop barking, such as "*Quiet,*" and reward him for being silent. In this way, you have control over when your Yorkie barks – and when he stops.

Humping cushions

A Yorkie puppy – male or female – may have a tendency to hump cushions, or even worse, a visitor's leg. This may begin in early puppyhood, and it may become more marked as the youngster hits adolescence. It is more likely to be seen in male Yorkies, but if a female is particularly dominant, she may exhibit the same behavior.

It is important to prevent this problem from becoming habitual. The first time you see your Yorkie humping a cushion, say "*No*" in a gruff, firm voice, and then withdraw your attention. Do not make a big issue of it, and whatever you do, do not laugh. A puppy does not understand what he is doing, but he will like the attention he is getting. Never reward a Yorkie's inappropriate behavior by giving him

attention. He will not understand that you are cross, upset, or embarrassed; he will be getting your undivided attention, which is what he wants.

It is important to balance negative correction with a positive reward. If you withdraw your attention when your Yorkie is misbehaving, you must find times to reward him by giving him your attention. Find the time to play with your Yorkie, run through some training exercises, or teach him some fun tricks. If your Yorkie's mind is occupied, he will have less time to indulge in inappropriate behavior.

If humping is tackled when the behavior first becomes apparent, and you adopt a firm, consistent approach, you will find that it soon ceases to be a problem.

Nipping

A Yorkie of good temperament should never show any hint of aggression. Although the terrier instinct is strong in the breed, this is characterized as feisty, fearless behavior; it has nothing to do with growling or biting.

The problem of nipping will arise if a puppy is not corrected when he first attempts to play-bite. This behavior is entirely natural among littermates. The puppies will play together, having mock fights, and in this way they learn about canine interaction. However, when your puppy arrives in his new home, and tries to mouth or bite your hand when you are handling him, you must put a stop to it right away. Your puppy has to learn that he must behave in a different, more respectful way when he is interacting with people. The best way of preventing nipping in a puppy is to practice giving treats, and teaching the puppy to take the reward "*Gently.*" Your puppy will soon learn that he will get the treat only if he takes it without grabbing or biting. In the same way, practice taking a toy from your puppy and exchanging it with a treat. Any self-respecting Yorkie will appreciate that he is being presented with a reasonable bargain, so he will learn to give up his toy on request. In addition, he will be learning how to interact with people in a controlled and civilized manner.

Occasionally, a Yorkie will resent being groomed or handled, and will show his disapproval by nipping. This is a potentially disastrous situation, particularly with a long-haired breed that needs regular grooming. It could also pose problems if your Yorkie needs to be examined by the veterinarian. Again, the secret is never to let the problem arise. If your puppy is used to being handled and groomed right from the start (see page 40), he will learn to accept the attention, and will even enjoy it. Do not attempt to groom a puppy for too lengthy a period, or he will become bored and fidgety, and always remember to reward good behavior with a treat or a game.

If an adult Yorkie is showing signs of resentment, you must start from scratch and treat the dog as if he was a puppy. Lay the brush on him for just a second, and then reward him. Touch his ear, or his tail, and then give a treat. Run your hand along the length of his body, and then tickle his tummy. Talk to your

Work at making grooming a pleasurable time, rewarding your dog after just a few strokes with the brush.

Yorkie in a calm, reassuring tone of voice, and this will encourage him to relax. After just a few minutes, end the session with a game so your Yorkie can run about and use up his pent-up energy.

If at any stage your Yorkie tries to struggle, growl, or nip, you must correct him instantly, with a firm "*No.*" Do not be tempted to end the grooming session at this stage. Your dog must not become the boss, dictating what he likes or doesn't like. You must be in control, and show him that you are not frightened by his growl. Speak to your dog firmly, handle him with confidence, and be swift to give a reward. Build up the length of handling and grooming sessions over a period of time, and your Yorkie will learn to accept the attention without resentment.

If you are concerned that you are not making progress with this problem, do not delay in seeking the help of a qualified animal behaviorist who will be able to give you expert guidance.

Possessiveness

Most Yorkies love playing with toys, and often seem to have a particular favorite among their collection. It is all too easy for a dog to become possessive of a toy, guarding it and refusing to give it up when asked. This may not seem like a major problem in itself, but it is important to look at the underlying cause.

The Yorkie likes to hang on to his toys – but he must learn to give them up on request.

If a Yorkie growls when you try to take his toy away, he is saying, "This is my toy, and you have no right to it." In order for the human/canine relationship to work, your dog must realize that he may have his toy only when you say so. If you ask him to give up his toy, he must do so without dissent. The reason why you must get on top of this situation is that your Yorkie is challenging you, saying he is the boss. He may show similar behavior if you approach his bed, or if you try to move him from the sofa.

Do not delay tackling this problem, as it can quickly escalate, and you will end up with a dog that is attempting to rule the roost. Try the following steps to re-educate your Yorkie and to remind him of his proper status within the family pack.

- Do not leave toys around so that your Yorkie can play with them at will. Bring them out at play sessions, and when you want your Yorkie to give up a toy, exchange it for a treat.
- Do not allow your Yorkie to sleep on the bed or on the sofa. In his eyes, his status is elevated by being allowed to choose where he sleeps.
- When your Yorkie is in his bed, approach him and give him a treat. Stroke him, and then leave him in peace. In this way, your Yorkie will learn not to be overprotective of his personal space.
- When you feed your Yorkie, drop in a couple of treats while he is eating so he welcomes

your interference and does not try to guard his food bowl. You can progress to taking his bowl away for a couple of seconds, and then giving it back to him with lots of praise.

- When you are going through doors, make sure you command your Yorkie to "*Wait,*" so that you always go through first.

In addition to these exercises, make sure you give your Yorkie plenty of mental stimulation in the form of training, playing games, and going on outings. The aim is to reinforce your leadership, but also to show the benefits that come if your Yorkie accepts the status quo.

Separation anxiety

A Yorkie is a wonderful companion, and he thrives on having human company. However, problems may arise if your Yorkie becomes too dependent on people and feels he cannot cope on his own. A dog that is suffering from separation anxiety may show a number of different types of behavior. He may:

- Bark or whine continuously when you are away.
- Become destructive.
- Soil his bed or the room in which he is left.

This is an upsetting problem for both dog and owner – and it is entirely avoidable. While your Yorkie is growing up, it is important that he gets used to being left for short periods. In this way, he will learn that there is nothing to worry about when he is alone, and, more importantly, he will discover that you always come back!

If your Yorkie is showing signs of distress when you leave him, do not feel sorry for him and decide that you should not go out. A dog that suffers from separation anxiety is not a happy animal, and you owe it to him to tackle the problem. There may be a time when you have to go away unexpectedly, and so it is important that your Yorkie becomes a little more self-reliant.

Try the following steps to ease your Yorkie's anxiety:

- If you have not done so already, invest in a crate, and work on crate-training (see page 35). Your Yorkie will learn to feel safe and secure in his own special den, which will lessen his anxiety. It will prevent

A crate is an essential aid in overcoming separation anxiety.

destructiveness, and it will also reduce the chance of soiling, as a dog does not like to foul his own bed.

- Use a childgate (stairgate) between rooms. Your Yorkie can be left alone, but he will still be able to see you.
- Buy some boredom-busting toys, where you can secrete food treats within the toy. Your Yorkie will be so busy trying to get at the food, he will not have time to miss you!
- Make a few mock departures, jangling your keys and putting on your coat. Leave your Yorkie for a few minutes and then return to him. This will teach him not to become hyped up every time he thinks you are going out.
- When you do go out, do not make a big fuss over him as you leave, or when you return. Wait for five minutes or so before you go to your Yorkie, and then behave in a calm, relaxed manner. If an owner gets emotional about arrivals and departures, it is quickly transmitted to the dog, who will become upset and distressed.

This is not a difficult problem to crack, as long as you stick to the guidelines suggested, and you do not get trapped into believing that your Yorkie cannot manage without you.

The Yorkie is an exceptionally sensitive dog, and he will quickly pick up on his owner's thoughts and feelings. The kind, responsible owner is the one who trains his pet to be calm and relaxed, and able to cope with short periods of solitude.

NEUTERING

If you do not plan to breed from your Yorkie, you may wish to consider the option of neutering. This can help to overcome behavioral problems and it also has a number of health benefits.

In males, the testicles are removed. This means a reduction in prostate disorders, and the risk of testicular cancer is eliminated.

In females, the surgery is more major, as it involves the removal of the womb. However, a spayed female will not develop pyometra, which is a life-threatening condition in which the womb fills with pus. The chance of a female Yorkie developing mammary tumors is also drastically reduced.

It is important that a Yorkie is physically mature before neutering. This applies equally to both males and females. It has been found that improvements in behavior are likely to occur only if a dog has achieved full physical maturity. Male Yorkies take a surprisingly long time to mature, and it would be wise to delay neutering until your dog is over 12 months of age. Some breeders believe a female should not be spayed until she has had her first season, but this negates much of the protection against mammary cancer. A female should be over six months of age, but, ideally, it should be done before her first season. It is a good idea to discuss the timing of the surgery with your veterinarian.

Neutering is a routine operation, and your Yorkie should make a swift recovery. Once your Yorkie is fully fit, you should talk to your veterinarian about your dog's dietary requirements. Neutering lowers

Discuss the pros and cons of neutering with your veterinarian.

hormone levels, and this can have an effect on the dog's metabolism. Your Yorkie may not need as much food as previously, or he may require a diet that is lower in calories.

Remember, Yorkies suffer major health problems if they become obese (see page 70), so listen to your veterinarian's advice, and make any changes he or she suggests.

SUMMING UP

Adolescence is not the easiest time for dog or owner, but there is no need for long-term problems to result. Be aware of your Yorkie's changing needs. Be ready to give him guidance and leadership. In no time, he will grow out of his teenage phase, and you will have a wonderful companion to share your life with.

CHAPTER SIX

CARING FOR YOUR YORKIE

Fun-loving and full of energy, the Yorkshire Terrier believes in living life to the full. He may be small in size, but this is a dog that wants to get involved with everything that is going on.

Do not make the mistake of treating your Yorkie like a pampered pooch that is incapable of taking exercise or of joining in with the family fun. Treat your Yorkie like a dog – and he will be the first to thank you for it.

FEEDING

An adult Yorkshire Terrier will need two meals a day. It is never easy to be specific about quantities, as this will depend on the size of the dog. However, as a general rule of thumb, the protein content of the meal should be half an ounce per pound of bodyweight (14 g per 0.45 kg).

Complete diets are probably the best method of feeding. There are diets made especially for Toy dogs – in the U.K. there is even a diet specifically for Yorkshire Terriers – and these will contain the correct nutritional balance for a small, but energetic, dog.

Most Yorkies appreciate a little cooked chicken, beef, or lamb to make the meal more appetizing. It is also a good idea to introduce some fiber in the diet, such as grated carrot or finely chopped cabbage. It does appear that Yorkies who eat a reasonable amount of fiber have fewer health problems and a better life expectancy.

If your Yorkie will eat hard biscuits, this is a great bonus, as it will help to keep his teeth clean and prevent the buildup of tartar. However, there are some Yorkies that show no interest in this type of food. If this is the case, try some dental chews, which your Yorkie may enjoy.

Fussy feeders

Yorkies can become fussy about their food, and there are some that have a poor appetite. There are various ways of tempting a reluctant feeder:

- Add some cooked chicken to the meal. Some Yorkies also like beef or lamb, but chicken is nearly always a favorite.
- Grate some cheese over the meal.
- Soak the meal in gravy.

If you have a fussy feeder, you may well find that whatever treat worked one week will probably be rejected the following week. If this happens, try to be inventive, and add variety to your dog's diet – grate a little carrot instead of using cheese, or change the type of meat you are offering. If you have more than one dog, feed them together, as this can produce some healthy rivalry.

Do not fuss over your Yorkie, or he will become a fussy feeder.

Try not to put too much pressure on your dog if he is being picky about his food. If you are not careful, you can take the problem too seriously, and your Yorkie will expect an even more tantalizing morsel every time he is fed. Although it is important to maintain a stable weight, no Yorkie has ever starved himself, so make sure you keep the problem in proportion.

Dangers of obesity

It is hard to imagine that the lively little puppy you brought home could ever become overweight. However, obesity is a serious problem in the breed, and it is one that is entirely preventable. A Toy dog that is given too much to eat will quickly put on excess pounds, and serious health problems will result. The Yorkie's mind is so active that he will still try to rush around, despite his excess weight, and this will put strain on his heart and his knees. In severe cases of obesity, liver and kidney failure may result.

Resist those pleading eyes, and think about your dog's well-being. It may help if you make a note of your dog's weight, and then keep a check on it, so you will be able to spot an increase at an early stage. A good test is to put your hand around your Yorkie's shoulders – this is the first place where he will put on weight. If your hand forms a V, your Yorkie is not overweight; if your fingers begin to spread and you are making more of a U shape, you know your dog is putting on too much weight.

If your Yorkie has become overweight, do not delay in seeking advice from your veterinarian.

The Yorkshire Terrier does not need a lot of exercise, but it is essential to provide mental stimulation.

There are a number of foods that are specially formulated for obese dogs; and your veterinarian will be able to give you suitable advice. Many veterinary practices now hold clinics for canine dieters, and these can help owners to implement a diet in a safe, sensible manner.

EXERCISE

While your puppy is growing, he will get as much exercise as he needs within the confines of your garden. When he has completed his vaccination course, you will be able to take him for short outings as part of his socialization program (see page 43). Remember that a puppy tires easily, so you should not make these expeditions too long. Lead-walking is especially grueling, so it is better to plan for ten-minute sessions while your puppy is growing.

How much exercise should you give an adult Yorkshire Terrier? The answer varies tremendously, depending on the age of both dog and owner, and the preferred lifestyle. A Yorkie is very adaptable, and, basically, he will make do with whatever exercise he is given. He will suit an elderly or infirm owner who cannot manage lengthy expeditions, and, equally, he is game enough to keep going for a good number of miles. There was one Yorkie that went on a sponsored walk, and most sponsors gave enough to cover the first half of the route. However, this little Yorkie had no intention of giving up early, and he completed the entire 12-mile course!

Obviously, this type of outing is an exception. However, it is important to remember that although a Yorkie does not need a daily marathon, he has high energy levels. This is a busy, active dog that rarely seems to tire. If you are not able to give your Yorkie a lot of exercise, you must provide him with mental stimulation. This can take the form of training exercises, retrieve games in the garden, or simply taking him for trips in the car, or a short walk to the local shops. As long as a Yorkie has variety in his life, and feels involved in his owner's activities, he will be content.

Grooming provides the ideal opportunity to give your Yorkie a thorough checkup.

ADULT GROOMING

We tend to think of grooming purely in terms of coat care, but actually, it applies to the overall care of a dog. A grooming session provides the opportunity to check eyes, ears, teeth, and nails, as well as brushing through the coat. It also gives you the chance to examine the dog.

If you are handling your Yorkie, you will be able to spot any unusual lumps or bumps, or any evidence of skin irritation. This is particularly important in a long-haired breed, when the coat can literally cover any sign of trouble. In all cases, a problem that is detected in its earliest stages will be far easier to resolve. The responsible dog owner should therefore see regular examinations as part of routine care. It is best to work in a logical order, starting at the head and progressing down the length of the body to the hindquarters, so that you do not miss anything.

The eyes

The eyes should be bright and sparkling, and there should be no sign of redness. Any debris can be wiped away, being sure to use a clean piece of cotton wool (cotton) for each eye. If there is any sign of persistent discharge, consult your veterinarian.

The ears

Check the ears. They should be clean and free from odor. If there is a little dirt, it can be wiped away, again using a fresh piece of cotton wool for each ear. Do not be tempted to probe into the ear canal, as you could do more harm than good.

Yorkies tend to grow hair inside the ear, and this will need to be trimmed. If you are new to Yorkie ownership, ask an experienced owner or breeder to help you with this.

The teeth

Toy dogs are not blessed with the best of teeth. There may be problems with the milk teeth failing to drop out, the adult teeth may become overcrowded, or the teeth may be shallow rooted (see Dental Problems, page 126). Keep a close check on your Yorkie's teeth, and if you have any concerns, consult your veterinarian.

It is vital to keep the teeth clean and the gums free from infection. This will make life more comfortable for your dog on a daily basis, and it will also help to prevent dental problems in later life. If there is a major accumulation of tartar, the veterinarian will have to tackle this under anesthesia. Yorkies can be vulnerable under anesthesia, so it is far better to prevent the situation from arising by paying attention to dental hygiene.

Regular brushing will keep the teeth clean and the gums healthy.

Trim the tips of the nails using guillotine nail clippers.

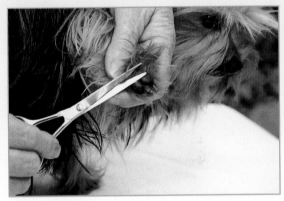

The hair growing between the pads will need to be trimmed.

Most Yorkies tolerate teeth-cleaning, particularly if they are accustomed to the routine from an early age. Canine toothpaste comes in a variety of meaty flavors, which most dogs find quite palatable. It may help if you start by smearing a little paste on your Yorkie's teeth, so that he realizes there is something in it for him! You can buy a long-handled toothbrush, or you can use a finger brush, and then work in the paste with an up-and-down motion. When you have finished, give your Yorkie lots of praise, and reward him with a treat. He will soon learn that teeth cleaning is not so bad – particularly if it ends with a treat.

Feet

If a dog is walked on hard surfaces, his nails may wear down naturally. However, most

Above: The puppy coat is black with tan markings.

Above right: At around four months, the blue color will begin to come through.

Right: The rich gold tan and steel blue coat of a Yorkie in full coat.

Yorkies need a little help to keep their nails in trim. Again, a puppy should be used to having his nails clipped, and so it will be a matter of simple routine.

It is important to trim the tip of the nail only, otherwise you risk cutting into the quick (the nerves and blood supply to the nail), which will bleed profusely. The best plan is to trim the nails regularly, and then you need to remove only a tiny amount. You can use scissors or nail clippers for this task. If you are worried about trimming nails, ask a nurse at the veterinary practice to give you a lesson.

You will also need to check the pads to ensure there are no cuts or cracks. This is particularly important if you take a walk in rough country, as it is easy for a thorn or a grass seed to become embedded in the pad. You will also need to trim the hair that grows between the pads, as this can become very uncomfortable for the dog. You may also like to make the appearance of the foot neat by trimming the hair around it.

Rear ends

It is a fact of life that the rear end of a long-haired breed can become messy after toileting.

It is essential that you keep a regular check, and clean up if necessary. You will not have to give a full-scale bath (see page 76), but just a quick wash and dry. This prevents your Yorkie from becoming smelly, and also prevents any soreness from developing in this area. Some owners trim the hair around the anus, which helps to keep the dog as clean as possible.

The Yorkie coat

Caring for your Yorkie's coat is one of the pleasures of owning this breed. There is a sizeable workload for the average pet owner, let alone for the exhibitor who keeps the coat at full length. However, if your puppy is accustomed to grooming from an early age, he will positively enjoy the experience. He will benefit from having one-on-one attention, and most Yorkie owners find grooming thoroughly therapeutic.

The puppy coat needs regular brushing and combing. Ideally, you should set aside time every day, but, at the very minimum, you should groom your puppy three times a week. An adult Yorkie should be groomed on a daily basis.

As your puppy grows, you will notice changes in the coat. From around 8–16 weeks, the black hair on top of the head will start to turn to a shade of mid-gray. From six months, this will begin to turn to tan. All dogs are different, but, generally, the color will develop gradually, and the true, rich tan color, which should resemble the color of an 18 carat gold wedding ring, should be apparent between 18 months and two years.

The body coat of a young puppy is black, but you will see the blue color coming through when the puppy is between four and six months of age. If the color is going to be a dark, steel blue, you will see the color coming through from where the tan coat finishes, and it will gradually spread down the body. A lighter steel color tends to break out all over the body. This is very much a gradual process, and will vary from dog to dog. In the show ring, a dog is considered to be in his prime, in terms of the color and length of coat, at around three years old. As the dog ages, the shade of the coat becomes progressively lighter.

The texture of the Yorkie coat is unique in the dog world. In fact, it is very much like human hair, and does not have the oiliness or odor that is characteristic of most breeds. The hair should feel fine to the touch – neither too soft, nor too harsh. Ideally, you should be able to run the coat between your finger and thumb, and feel every individual hair.

The Yorkie does not have an undercoat, but he is such an active little dog that he seems to have no problem keeping warm. The coat does not shed, although some puppies may lose some hair as the adult coat is coming through. This is not a dramatic occurrence, but you may see some hairs in the brush when you have finished grooming. The coat grows continuously, and this needs to be kept in check, either by clipping or scissoring. Even if a Yorkie is kept in full coat, the length will need to be trimmed; otherwise the dog is unable to move freely.

Bathing

With the majority of dog breeds, it is recommended to keep bathing to a minimum in order to retain the natural oils in the coat. The Yorkie's coat is free from oils, and so it needs to be treated like human hair and washed frequently. A Yorkie will need bathing at least every two weeks, and many owners get into the routine of bathing on a weekly basis. This sounds like hard work, but if your Yorkie is used to the routine, he will not put up a fight. The advantage of bathing a small breed is that you can use the sink, so the task does not need to be backbreaking.

The best plan is to get everything ready before you get your dog wet! You will need a dog shampoo, a conditioner, a jar for mixing the conditioner, and lots of towels.

- Start by brushing and combing the coat to be sure it is free from mats or tangles. These will be very hard to tease out once the coat is wet.
- Place a rubber mat in the sink, which will stop your Yorkie from slipping. Fix a shower appliance to the taps, and run the water until it is luke warm.
- Wet the coat thoroughly, making sure you do not get water in the eyes or ears. You can use cotton wool earplugs to be on the safe side.
- Apply the shampoo and work into the coat, using a gentle massaging motion. Do not rub the hair, or it will get tangled.
- Rinse the coat, making sure you remove all traces of shampoo.

- Dilute the conditioner in a jar, and pour it over the coat. Again, work the conditioner into the coat.
- Rinse thoroughly, allowing the water to run through the coat until it is completely clear.
- Use a towel to absorb as much moisture as possible, before lifting your Yorkie out of the sink. Allow him to shake, and then wrap him in a fresh, dry towel.
- Use a hairdryer, on a moderate setting, to dry the coat. As you dry, brush through the coat, leaving it clean, dry, and tangle-free.

THE PET YORKIE

When your Yorkie becomes an adult, you will have to decide what you are going to do with his coat. The rule of thumb is to make a choice that will suit your lifestyle. If you like walking, and you want your Yorkie to accompany you on walks in the country, it is impractical to allow the coat to grow. The inevitable result will be a coat that is full of mats and tangles, which will cause both you and your dog no end of trouble. In this situation, the best plan is to keep the coat clipped.

Find a groomer who is used to clipping Yorkies, and decide on the best coat length. It will then be a matter of brushing and combing through the coat at least three times a week, and bathing on a weekly basis or every two weeks. In most cases, the coat will need to be clipped every three months.

Some owners like to keep a reasonable length of coat, but they do not want all the work associated with keeping a Yorkie in full coat.

PET GROOMING

The coat needs to be brushed through, layer by layer.

Get your Yorkie in a comfortable position to brush his underside.

Work along the body, finishing at the hindquarters.

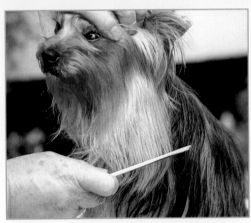

Repeat the whole process, using a wide-toothed comb.

Secure the head coat in a topknot.

This can be achieved by scissoring the coat to a length that is practical for everyday life. It is best to use the services of a professional groomer, so that your Yorkie looks smart. The groomer will scissor the coat in layers, and then trim the length. Obviously, the length of coat you choose will affect how frequently it needs to be scissored.

It is important to remember that once the Yorkie's coat has been clipped or scissored into layers, it will not grow to its full length.

Regardless of how long you allow the coat to grow, your Yorkie will need to be groomed every day. If you do this, the job takes only a few minutes, but if you leave it longer, you will have mats and tangles to contend with.

- Start by brushing through the coat with a bristle brush. It does not matter where you start, or where you finish – most Yorkie owners work to their own routine.
- It will help if you work through the coat in layers, brushing it a layer at a time.
- You will need to get to your Yorkie's underside. This can be done with the dog lying on a table, or you can take him on to your lap and let him lie against you as you brush the coat.
- Use a wide-toothed comb to work through the coat. If you come across any mats, these can be gently teased out. Pay particular attention to the hair behind the ears, which mats very easily. You also need to work on the hair around the face, as this can become matted with food.

- The hair on top of the head will need to be tied in a topknot. This is done by combing the hair forward, smoothing it backward, and then securing it with an elastic band. In the show ring, a red ribbon is traditionally tied in a bow around the topknot. Pet owners can use a clip or a ribbon, depending on personal preference.
- Always reward your Yorkie at the end of a grooming session, so that he learns to enjoy these special times he spends with you.

THE SHOW DOG

If a Yorkie is to be shown in the ring, he will need to be kept in full coat. This involves a huge amount of work, and there are few pet owners who decide on this option.

As the coat becomes longer, it needs to be protected, otherwise it is easily torn or damaged. This is done by keeping the hair in papers (sometimes referred to as crackers or wraps). These are sheets of acid-free tissue paper, which are literally wrapped around the strands of the coat. The paper is then folded over into a neat package, and secured with a rubber band. The hair is oiled before it is put into papers, in order to keep it lubricated.

If a dog is kept in papers, he will need daily attention. The papers need to be taken out every day, so that the coat can be brushed through, and then the papers need to be replaced. You can fit the dog in a coat, which helps to keep the papers in place. Some people also use boots so that if the Yorkie scratches, he does not ruin all your hard work! Obviously, papers get loose

THE SHOW DOG

Tissue is used to protect the long coat.

The hair is wrapped in a package and folded over.

The hair is secured in a neat package.

The body hair and the tail also need to be protected.

A Yorkie in full coat can still enjoy freedom.

during the course of the day, particularly around the head, and so these may need extra attention. In addition, a Yorkie in full coat will need a weekly bath, plus routine care on his ears, eyes, teeth, and nails.

Keeping a Yorkie in full coat is a job for the dedicated few – but there is no doubt that the end result is magnificent. It is also important to realize that a Yorkie in full coat is still a real dog, and should be allowed to run around and play. If his coat is in papers, he will not do it any damage – and it is every dog's right to be given a reasonable degree of freedom.

For information on preparing a Yorkie for the show ring, see page 109.

THE VETERAN YORKIE

We are lucky that Yorkies are a long-lived breed, and most will survive into their teens. It seems that the medium-sized and larger Yorkies are generally stronger, and are more likely to live to an old age than tiny dogs who weigh 4 pounds (1.8 kg) or less.

Many Yorkies remain young at heart throughout their lives, and still like playing with toys in their veteran years. However, it is important that, as your dog grows older, you are aware of his changing needs.

The most important consideration is diet. Your Yorkie will be less active as he ages, and so he will need a change of diet. There are a number of complete diets that are specially formulated for veteran dogs, and this may be a sensible choice. You may find that your elderly Yorkie prefers to eat a little at a time, and three small meals a day may be preferable to dividing his ration into two meals. Make sure you keep a close check on your dog's weight, and consult your veterinarian if there is any marked departure from the norm.

Allow your Yorkie to decide how much exercise to take. Some dogs stay more active than others, so it is a matter of monitoring your dog and making sure he does not become over-tired. Equally, it is important that your Yorkie does not become a couch potato, so even if he does not want to go far, make sure you take him for short outings.

EUTHANASIA

Inevitably, there comes a time when your Yorkie becomes ill, or his body simply gives up on him. This is the time to be brave, and to make the decision to end your dog's life with the minimum of suffering. All too often, an owner cannot bear to let go, and the dog ends his life in discomfort, and perhaps even more importantly, without dignity.

When the time comes, be prepared to show your beloved pet a last true act of kindness, and let him slip away without pain or suffering. Obviously you will miss your old friend for many months, but, in time, you will recall all the happy times you spent together, and you will get some comfort from your memories.

Take the time you need to get over your loss, and, hopefully, you will then be ready to pay your Yorkshire Terrier the greatest compliment of all – going out and getting a new Yorkie puppy…

LETTING GO OF MISTER

Rose Edwards from Baraga, Michigan, has kept Yorkies for many years. In that time, Rose has had to make the difficult decision whether or not to euthanize her beloved pets when their lives have become unbearable through illness.

"I keep several Yorkies, and I adore their personality and their size. At home, my Yorkies have a rubber ball that they play with, which they balance on their noses and chase around the yard like seals at a circus. I love to watch them and I can't imagine life without them.

"I had one particular Yorkie – Rose's Hey Mister – that I was particularly fond of, but, sadly, he died before he reached one year of age. I acquired Hey Mister when he was just 11 weeks old, and quickly formed a strong bond with him. However, it was quickly apparent that something wasn't right. He suffered terrible seizures and I spent months running to and from the veterinarian's, trying all sorts of medication and accumulating huge bills. I was prepared to try anything for Hey Mister.

"One day, I came home and found him hiding in my boot having a terrible seizure. He was soaking all over because he had been foaming at the mouth so much, and his body was contorted from the terrible pain he was in. I rushed him to the veterinarian, all the time thinking that no way could I subject any living animal to this sort of existence. I knew he would have no kind of life to speak of and that allowing him to continue living this kind of life was going to be too hard for us both. That seizure was the last.

"I missed Hey Mister dreadfully, and my other Yorkies did too. They know when something has happened. I remembered when I lost another Yorkie, Lacy, and I buried her in the backyard, along with a few cultural items in keeping with my Native American background. It was a very solemn occasion and my Yorkies – who normally go mad with excitement when they are let out to play in the yard – lined up on the porch, watching me bury Lacy. They were very quiet for a few days, almost as if they were mourning. It brought us even closer and my remaining Yorkies helped to ease the pain of losing one, very much-loved pet.

"Although it was heartbreaking for me, I knew, deep down in my heart, that I and my veterinarian had done everything possible for Hey Mister – there was nothing left to try. After he had passed away, we discovered that he had liver shunt, and this had been responsible for the terrible seizures he had suffered from. There was nothing that could have been done for him, and I know now that I made the right decision. The only advice I could give to someone in a similar situation is to look into your heart and think about what is best for your pet and for you."

Yorkies have always been an important part of Rose's family.

CHAPTER SEVEN

THE VERSATILE YORKIE

Although the Yorkie is kept mainly as a companion, his larger-than-life personality belies his diminutive size, and his intelligence and friendly character make him well suited to further training. The range of activities suitable for your Yorkie is not as limited as you first may think, given his size. Many sports can be adapted to suit smaller dogs, as our case study on Agility shows. There is something to suit almost everyone, and, by becoming involved in a new hobby, you and your Yorkie will have a great deal of fun together.

CANINE GOOD CITIZEN

The Yorkshire Terrier has too lively a disposition to be a mere lapdog, and, like all breeds, he should be taught good manners and how to behave appropriately in a variety of everyday situations. To this end, the "Good Citizen" program is an excellent way to improve on your Yorkie's initial puppy training and socialization.

In the U.K., the program is known as the Good Citizen Dog Scheme, run by the British Kennel Club. The American Kennel Club (AKC) equivalent is the Canine Good Citizen Program. Both programs aim to encourage responsible dog ownership through education and training. To receive his Canine Good Citizen award, your dog will need to:

- Accept handling and grooming
- Respond to basic obedience commands
- Meet another dog in a friendly fashion
- Walk on a loose lead in a controlled manner
- Walk confidently through a crowd of people
- Accept being approached and petted by a stranger.

To find out more about these programs, contact your national kennel club.

OBEDIENCE

If your Yorkie responded well to his initial puppy training, you may want to try taking things a step further with Obedience. While the Yorkie is not the first breed to spring to mind

SUPER DOG SAMMY

Deborah Nendell, from Magna in Utah, began Obedience with her Yorkie, Sammy, 13 years ago. Sammy's achievements include being awarded his Canine Good Citizen award, and his Utility Dog and Tracking Dog titles.

"I had grown up around dogs, but until I got Sammy, I hadn't had a dog for more than 11 years. It all started because my sister got a rather wild little Sheltie, and she decided to take her to Obedience classes. I was really impressed, and, at Christmas, when I got Sammy, I began taking him to Obedience classes. He's been going ever since.

"Sammy excelled at Obedience right from the start. To begin with, I was quite shy and withdrawn, but Sammy played to his 'audience'

Super Dog Sammy: A hard act to follow.
Photo courtesy: Vavra Photography.

(the rest of the class) so much, I quickly became convinced that Obedience was great fun for us both. Every exercise he was shown, he got the first time. I try to make training as much fun as possible, making it a 'special time' for Sammy. He loves it because he gets lots of praise and treats when he gets something right. I also think it is very important to make sure that he is corrected in a fair manner. Yorkies can be very unforgiving if you treat them badly, so you need to make sure your dog knows why he hasn't got the reward or the treat. If he doesn't, he could well refuse to try again!

"Because Sammy was trained in a positive, reward-based fashion, he has done really, really well at Obedience. He was the first-ever Yorkie to achieve his AKC Utility Dog title in Utah, and he was the first multi-registry title holder to earn a Companion Dog title under ASCA. He's earned his Super Utility title as well, by qualifying in Open and Utility on the same day. Although there are many traditional Obedience breeds that are far larger than Sammy, he has the biggest and bravest heart of them all. His courage, commitment, and ability really shine when he's performing in competition. He's never let me down.

"Sammy's nickname is Super Dog, and he will be a hard act to follow. However, I'm now training my second Yorkie in Obedience, Parker. In his first year, he has already won nine titles. However, I'm not in Obedience for the titles. I take part because the dogs love it and I am able to show off their wonderful temperaments to others.

"I've been told by many people that Yorkies are stubborn and that I've been wasting my time trying to get Sammy to participate in performance sports, such as Obedience. However, I've found that Yorkies are much smarter than many people realize and they have brilliant personalities.

"Every dog needs a job, and, with the right trainer and the right motivation, Yorkies can excel at anything."

when thinking of Obedience, those that have taken up the sport have performed very well. However, training any breed of dog for Obedience competition requires commitment and hard work, and, if you are a highly competitive person, you should consider another breed. That said, there is a great deal of enjoyment to be gained from competing in Obedience (even if you do not win), and, of course, there is the added advantage of being the proud owner of an extremely well-behaved dog.

If Obedience appeals to you, you will need to join a training club. Your national kennel club will be able to provide you with details of clubs in your area.

AGILITY

Agility is one of the most popular of all canine sports. It is a type of obstacle course for dogs, and, although many people compete seriously, the emphasis is very definitely on having fun. It is the ideal sport to take up if you and your Yorkie have never tried any type of further training before.

To complete an Agility course, dogs must successfully negotiate a series of obstacles, within a set time and with no faults. The winner is the dog that has the fastest time with the least mistakes. The obstacles include hurdles, long jumps, tunnels and chutes, poles the dog must weave through, a seesaw or "teeter," a dog walk (a narrow, elevated walkway), and an A-frame (a steep, A-shaped ramp).

Agility is perfect for Yorkies, as this busy breed loves nothing more than racing through

The Yorkie is fast on his feet and loves the challenge of Agility.

tunnels and tackling obstacles at speed. Many Yorkies that take part in the sport race around the course so quickly that they are visible only as a black-and-tan blur! In America, where there is a stronger tradition of Toy breeds participating in Agility, Yorkies have acquitted themselves excellently.

Although Agility is enormous fun, it is a fairly demanding physical activity for both dog and handler, so, before taking up the sport, you will need to ensure that both you and your Yorkie are fit and healthy. You should also bear in mind that the kennel clubs of most countries refuse to allow puppies or growing dogs to take part. This is because the demanding nature of some obstacles can damage growing joints. Your national kennel club will tell you of the age restrictions in your country, as well as providing you with details of Agility clubs in your area.

MADISYN'S MOMENTS

Kathy Doheny's Yorkie, Madisyn, has been competing in Agility competitions for about three years. Here, Kathy describes why Madisyn loves the sport so much.

"Madisyn is my little ball of energy, and we were already participating in Flyball. My Flyball instructor also trained for Agility, and I thought it might be something Madisyn would like to try. I went along to an Agility trial to see what it was like and I found everyone to be really helpful and friendly. After that, Madisyn and I were hooked – I am now an official Agility junkie!

"Madisyn loves Agility, although it takes a lot of commitment and training. Madisyn is very well trained in basic obedience exercises, but we have to take classes once a week to work on different Agility obstacles, such as working at a distance or practicing the weave poles. The weaving poles are the most difficult obstacle for Madisyn.

"Generally, Madisyn has no problems with an Agility course, although she has had an unconventional approach at times. I remember one trial where she kept trying to jump over the tunnel, instead of running through it! I ended up laughing so much that I had to leave. Another time, we were the first pair to run the course and it was first thing in the morning. I couldn't remember the course layout – which order the

A "high five" on the table.

obstacles had to be tackled in – and I was panicking as I placed Madisyn on the starting line. I needn't have worried! Madisyn just took off, running and jumping over things. I tried to catch her but she was off and away and I could do nothing but watch her. Eventually, some spectators helped me to catch her.

"Madisyn thinks of Agility as an opportunity to play, which is why she loves the sport so much. She gets excited if I even mention the word Agility. Although we compete, and Madisyn has achieved her Elite Title in agility, the emphasis should be on fun. Yorkies can do well in Agility but you have to be patient and make it enjoyable for the dog. If you push too hard, you'll lose the dog's interest."

Shooting out of the tunnel.

FLYBALL

Flyball is a canine relay race. Two teams of four dogs compete and the winner is the team that finishes first. A Flyball track is 51 feet (15.5 meters) long, with four hurdles spaced evenly along it, and there are two identical tracks, one for each team.

Each dog runs the length of the track, jumping the four hurdles on the way. At the end of the track is a Flyball box, which the dog must trigger to release a ball. The dog has to catch the ball in his mouth, and then race back to the start of the track, jumping the hurdles again on his return journey.

When the first dog returns, the second dog is released, and so on until all the dogs have run.

RACY ROSIE

Doreen Smith and her five-year-old Yorkie, Rosie, have been participating in Flyball events for many years. Rosie is one of only a handful of Yorkies worldwide competing in the sport, and she has only one eye, but, as Doreen describes here, this does not stop her racing down the Flyball track!

"I first saw Flyball at the training club I went to with my Border Collies, Mork and Mindy. When I learned about a Flyball training course in Yorkshire, I couldn't resist finding out what it was all about. What a revelation! I was hooked for life, and I dashed home to set up my very own Flyball team, The Northern Bytes.

"I've had Rosie since she was a puppy and she is my second Yorkie – a breed to which I am fast becoming addicted. She lost her eye after an accident, which damaged her eye so badly it had to be removed. This doesn't hinder her in her quest to enjoy life – Rosie is a dog that knows what she wants and is prepared to do pretty much anything to achieve her goals!

"Rosie adores Flyball, although it took some time for her to learn the rules. Yorkshire Terriers are extremely intelligent, but you won't get them to do anything without the right motivation for the dog and an enormous amount

Rosie: A fast and determined Flyball competitor.

of determination from the trainer. It took ages for her to learn the retrieve, the mainstay of Flyball, but once she had, she's never looked back. A quick word of warning to other would-be Flyball competitors, however – the most likely motivation for a Yorkie is food, so make sure you deduct your training food from your dog's daily allowance. Don't end up with an overweight dog you have to put on a ▶

RACY ROSIE

diet – it won't gain you any 'grovel' points from your dog!

"Whenever Rosie and I train or compete, I have a ready supply of treats, as Rosie refuses to work unless you 'pay' her – she knows her rights. 'No pay, no play' is definitely her motto. I think this is why Rosie prefers Flyball to Agility, the sport she learned first. She has to do less work for her treats in Flyball. Unfortunately, her gritty determination to play the game correctly at all costs – to get the treat at the end – can sometimes lead her into trouble.

"She caused a bit of an upset at one Flyball competition when the ball bounced out of the box at a funny angle and shot across to the other team's lane. In Rosie's mind, finding the ball is the only way to get the biscuit.

"She flew across to the opposing team's lane and snatched the ball right from under the paws of the most enormous Border Collie! The Collie was so stunned, he stopped in his tracks to watch, in amazement, as this diminutive interloper dashed back to her own lane, hopped over the jumps, and was duly awarded her biscuit for winning the race. A brilliant moment of true victory!

"Rosie is one of the stars of British Flyball. Spectators come from far and wide to watch her, and she often outshines bigger, stronger dogs.

"Tipping the scales at a mere 7 pounds (3 kg) in weight, and standing about 9 inches at the shoulder (23 cm), she's one of the smallest dogs competing in Flyball anywhere in the world.

"The British Flyball Association awards points every time a dog successfully completes a 'leg' in a Flyball competition – and points make prizes. Rosie is the first Yorkie in the U.K. ever to reach the Silver Award for achieving 10,000 points.

"This is a landmark award that many dogs never reach. Our next goal is the Gold Award for 15,000 points – something we hope to gain with continued support from the rest of the team, Border Collies Tara and Kodi, and crossbreed Oggie. Mind you, I doubt Rosie will be content with this. No doubt, she'll set her sights on the Blue (20,000) or even the Platinum (25,000). The sky's the limit for this little girl!

"People tend to regard Yorkies as lapdogs, but they're capable of just about anything and never seem to notice that they're smaller than the rest of the canine world.

"Rosie is a dog with attitude, showing once and for all that a Yorkie can do whatever it wants to do!"

If a ball is dropped, or if a hurdle is missed or knocked, the dog must run the course again after the last member of the team has run.

Flyball is extremely popular in both the U.S. and the U.K. Again, the sport is dominated by large breeds, but many Toy breeds take part with a great deal of success, especially in America. However, Yorkies are very small dogs, so you will need to find a training club that is geared up for Toy breeds. Many clubs provide specially adapted boxes and smaller-sized tennis balls for Toy breeds.

To find out details of your nearest suitable club, contact your national kennel club.

FREESTYLE

Canine Freestyle, or Heelwork to Music, is a form of Obedience set to music. Dogs perform a series of Obedience maneuvers (e.g., the Sendaway) cleverly choreographed to music so that dog and handler appear to dance together. At national dog shows, such as Crufts in the U.K., Freestyle demonstrations are performed to an audience, without the element of competition. These performances are often televised, and if you have ever seen one on television, you cannot fail to be impressed.

There are numerous organizations involved with Freestyle, each with their own competition rules, although these are similar across clubs. Most performances last less than five minutes, and marks are awarded for two areas of the performance:

- Technical: this assesses accuracy, the synchronization between dog and owner, and the degree of difficulty in the routine.
- Presentation: this covers costume and the artistic flair shown in the choreography.

Freestyle is one of the most demanding of activities you can do with your Yorkie, and a fairly high level of obedience training is needed. The professionals make their performances appear seamless, but Freestyle is as demanding as traditional Competitive Obedience, and choreographed sequences, which take time to learn, combined with the added distraction of music, means that you will need a strong rapport with your Yorkie. That said, Freestyle is enormous fun, and dogs love it. Contact your national kennel club for more information.

THE PINK BUBBLE

Susan Colledge's 11-year-old Yorkie, Misha, has become one of the most famous Freestyle dogs around. Here, Susan describes how it all started.

"I had never heard of Freestyle before, but I am interested in everything to do with dogs, so I attended a seminar given by Joan Tennille, a cofounder of the Canine Freestyle Federation (CFF). It was an excellent presentation and I decided

Misha brings something special to Freestyle.

Freestyle was something I would like to try – it really shows the bond between dog and handler.

"It was quite difficult for me to get started, because there were no Freestyle clubs in Utah – only about five people in the entire state had heard of the sport! I had almost given up on the idea when Joan telephoned me and asked me if I would like to be in a demonstration at the American Kennel ▶

► Club Invitational in St. Louis. She needed a little dog and she had remembered Misha from the seminar I had attended.

"Freestyle is founded in Obedience, and Misha's Obedience moves were fine, but I was much weaker when it came to choreographing a dance. Fortunately, Joan helped me to choreograph our first routine.

"I practiced with Misha for five weeks before flying to St. Louis to perform. I was very nervous but Misha brought the house down. Everyone kept talking about 'the Yorkie, the Yorkie, the Yorkie.'

The finale of Misha's routine.

"From that one performance, Misha became something of a star. I couldn't believe how much of a lasting impact our two-minute dance had made. Since then, I have established a Freestyle training class. At the moment, I have about six members, and we meet once a week.

NATURAL RHYTHM

"One of the hardest aspects about Freestyle is finding a piece of music to work to. Everything in Freestyle is done to showcase the dog, so the music must suit the dog in question – matching the dog's natural rhythm. Misha is so tiny that our pieces must be very light, with flutes and jigs, etc., about 115 beats per minute. Bass guitars and heavy drumbeats would not suit her at all. Misha's performances are very different from a St. Bernard's, for example.

"Even within the same breed, each dog is very different. I train with another Yorkie, Tessa, whose dances are very different from Misha's. Misha is very 'airborn' in her routines, whereas Tessa is more 'earthbound.' It is one of the reasons I love Freestyle so much – it is the only sport that emphasizes each dog's uniqueness.

"Often, the dogs end up choosing their own music, and I think this is one of the reasons why Freestyle has such an emotional effect on audiences. Every performance Misha gives leaves the entire house – men included – in tears. We've been told we should provide boxes of tissues!

"Misha is that 'one-in-a-million' dog, my forever dog, and there will never be another like her. However, any Yorkie – or any dog of any breed for that matter – can do Freestyle. It depends on the individual dog and finding the right method of training.

"Misha adored the sport from the very start. Whenever she hears her music she gets really excited, and I've found that most dogs react in the same way.

"The most important thing to remember is to listen to the dog. For example, if you are training a particular move and the dog keeps performing it differently from what you want, the dog is probably right! It's all about trust and bonding.

"If you listen to your dog, you can produce some spellbinding routines. Misha and I have had occasions when we've entered what I call 'the pink bubble.' It's as if we become one – the world does not exist, except for our two souls uniting with the music.

OTHERWISE ENGAGED

"Misha has performed countless times now, and was recently honored by the Canine Freestyle Federation as being the dog that has done most for Freestyle. Her videos have been seen in Canada, England (including at Crufts), Australia, and several European countries. She performed at the AKC Invitational for three years in a row (the only dog to give repeat performances), not to mention numerous Nationals.

"She was even invited to perform at the World Dog Show in Ontario, Canada, but we had to decline because she was otherwise engaged – acting as Toto in a stage production of *The Wizard of Oz* – she brought the house down, yet again!

"Misha does limited performances now, as her age – she is 11 – is catching up with her. She has lost a lot of her hearing and had both her knees operated on. She is so in tune with me that she can perform without hearing the music very well, but it is a hindrance for learning new routines.

EMOTIONAL EXPERIENCE

"I'll never forget a performance she gave in Los Angeles about six months after her knee operation. I honestly didn't know if she would ever be able to dance again, but she gave one of the best performances of her life. It was an incredibly emotional experience.

"I'd advise anyone to have a go at Freestyle. Not only is it a great way to bond with your dog, but you also make some great new friends. Get to know your dog, decide what kind of music will suit their personality, look for unique movements, and find other interested people so that you can work together. Most of all, enjoy the bond you will develop with your dog. After a performance, I am always told by people, 'She [Misha] loves you so much,' and I always reply, 'Not half as much as I love her!'"

A SPECIAL BOND

The Yorkie excels as a companion dog, and, because of this, many people make the mistake of assuming that he is suited to nothing more than a life of idle companionship. However, there are several working avenues that really make the most of the Yorkie's affectionate and spirited disposition. Most people think of Golden Retrievers or Labradors when they think of dogs that help the disabled, but there is no reason why Yorkies cannot do just as good a job. Dogs for disabled, blind, or deaf people, however, are trained from puppyhood, and are usually specially chosen as puppies, but, if this sort of work appeals to you, and you think your Yorkie would enjoy the experience, why not become involved with therapy work, bringing joy to those who would otherwise have no contact with animals?

Assistance dogs

There are currently many types of assistance dog, working with a variety of people – from the blind and the deaf, to those who are disabled or handicapped.

The dog's role is to fill the gaps created by the owner's disability, whether that is alerting a deaf owner to the fact that the doorbell has just rung, or helping a handicapped person to put on their socks.

DEDICATED DAISY

Vonnie Truscott of Exeter, Devon, got more than she bargained for with her tiny little Yorkie Daisy…

"I have been going deaf steadily over the last 27 years. Daisy is my hearing dog, from Hearing Dogs for Deaf People, and I have had her since October 2001. Daisy is the smallest hearing dog ever to be trained by HDDP, but she doesn't seem to let this get in the way – her personality is 10 times larger than her body!

"Like all hearing dogs, Daisy was taught to alert me to a wide variety of sounds, one of which was the smoke alarm. Not long after I had her, her training was put to the test. I was cooking bacon in the kitchen when Daisy came racing in and jumped up at me. I asked her what the matter was and she immediately dropped to the floor. I was a little worried because I knew this meant danger, but when a neighbor told me my smoke alarm was going off, I just assumed the bacon had set it off and I thought no more about it.

"Unfortunately, what I didn't realize at the time was that my smoke alarm had a direct connection to the fire station. A few moments after the initial panic, which I now thought was over, Daisy came dashing up to me again, trying to get me to walk over to the window. When I did, I couldn't believe my eyes. Two fire engines and 12 burly firefighters were standing in my driveway! Fortunately, the firefighters saw the funny side of things, and no real harm was done – it is far better to be safe than sorry.

"I am very, very proud that I was fortunate enough to receive such a helpful, loving, funny, and faithful little friend, and I count myself extremely lucky to have Daisy as my miniature hearing aid. I feel secure in the knowledge that if a real fire happens, Daisy will look after me."

Daisy: A faithful, loving, and funny friend.

In recent years, more Yorkies have taken up roles as assistance dogs, although the field remains dominated by traditional assistance breeds, such as the Labrador Retriever and the Golden Retriever. One role in which Yorkies really excel, however, is as hearing dogs for the deaf. As our case histories show, the Yorkshire Terrier's affectionate and larger-than-life personality can make a real difference to a deaf owner's quality of life.

THE BEST BUDDY

Addie Miller, from Las Vegas, got her first Yorkie, Buddy, three-and-a-half years ago. Buddy is a hearing dog, and he helps Addie cope with everyday things that her hearing impairment makes difficult. Here, she describes the difference Buddy has made to her life.

"I have suffered from a hearing impairment for about 20 years. I have severe loss in my left ear and I am profoundly deaf in the right. When I applied for a hearing dog, I asked for a small dog that did not shed much hair. This turned out to be Buddy, a Yorkshire Terrier, and I've loved the breed ever since.

"Before I could take Buddy, I had to be assessed by Dogs for the Deaf, who wanted to ensure that my lifestyle and home environment were suitable for a dog. I also had to be taught how to understand what Buddy was telling me, which involved five full days of hands-on learning. Buddy was trained to alert me to various sounds, including the doorbell, the telephone, someone calling my name, the smoke alarm, and even my cooker timer. Every day, we learn something new together, and he has

Hearing Dog Buddy has made a huge difference.

become an invaluable part of my life.

"Buddy has made a huge difference to my confidence and feelings of security. Before I had Buddy I used to miss people calling at my door or on the telephone, and I frequently overslept. I used to be terrified of missing important meetings at work. I was afraid to go to sleep at night, because, once I had removed my hearing aid, I couldn't hear a thing. Having Buddy has changed all that. He is my lifeline to the world and he is also a wonderful companion – smart, funny, and a good listener. I go out for the evening now, because I am confident I will be able to cope with Buddy by my side.

"Since I acquired Buddy, we have become inseparable – if I have to be away from him for a day or two, I feel like a part of me is missing. He has made such a difference to my quality of life that I would like to see far more hearing dogs available to deaf people. Buddy and I regularly hold education workshops to educate people about what it is like to be deaf, and how hearing dogs can help. These dogs give their owners so much independence, allowing them to live less restricted lives."

Therapy dogs

Loyalty, devotion, and a love of life – these are all attributes the Yorkie possesses. He is easy to train, cheerful, and friendly. These qualities, combined with his ability to get along with everyone, make him ideally suited to work as a therapy dog.

Sadly, many people live a life deprived of contact with animals, made worse because many are lifelong animal lovers who greatly miss the companionship provided by their pets. For example, many of the elderly in residential homes often find that the absence of animal companionship adds to their feelings of isolation and loneliness. In other cases, people's disabilities or circumstances have prevented them from ever experiencing the joy of dog ownership (e.g., residents of children's homes or homes for the severely disabled). It is people such as these who benefit from regular contact with a therapy dog.

Therapy dogs visit a variety of establishments, including residential homes, schools in deprived areas, hospitals and hospices, and prisons. The schemes are becoming increasingly popular in the U.K. and the U.S. This is due, in no small part, to the fact that contact with pets is extremely beneficial to our health and mental well-being, reducing stress, boosting the immune system, and giving pleasure simply through companionship.

Therapy dog programs rely on an army of volunteers and their pets. To become a therapy dog, your Yorkie will need to be character-assessed by one of the therapy dog organizations in your country. All therapy dogs must be totally trustworthy, and comfortable in unfamiliar surroundings and the company of strangers. This is why the Good Citizen Program, (see page 83) is so important – it is a stepping stone to all sorts of interesting and rewarding activities.

Yorkies thrive on attention, and, in addition, you will have the reward of knowing that you have brought a great deal of pleasure into the lives of many people. To find out more, contact your national kennel club for details about therapy dog organizations, or try browsing the Internet.

Education programs

It is a sad fact that cruelty to animals seems to be on the increase, and we have all seen cases reported in the national press. However, there is a small army of volunteers dedicated to reversing this trend. The pro-dog program aims to educate children about the responsibilities of dog ownership and how to approach dogs in the right fashion. It is hoped that, over time, the programs will result in a new generation of people who are comfortable around dogs, and who will be responsible owners should they have their own dogs in the future.

Mostly, handlers take their dogs to schools, where children can be educated informally, in a comfortable and familiar environment, and where the handler can ensure that no harm comes to the dog.

If this work appeals to you, your national kennel club will be able to provide you with details about the program.

MIRACULOUS MILO

Jean Astbury, from Coventry, Warwickshire, has kept Yorkies for more than 20 years. She has been involved with therapy dogs for 10 years. Here, she recounts some of her experiences with one of her Yorkies, Milo.

"I began doing therapy work some years before the Pets As Therapy (PAT) program was launched in the U.K. However, a little while after the PAT dog program was established, I visited Crufts, where PAT had a stall. As I had experience, and because I had always enjoyed the work, I decided to register Toby, my Yorkie at the time.

"I visit residential homes once a week, as well as a number of schools. Although the work is very time-consuming, especially when you have to travel to places, it is enormously rewarding.

"I have had some incredibly moving experiences. For example, I once visited a lady who had not spoken for more than three years. When I placed Milo on her lap, she didn't stop talking for the next hour and a half! A similar event happened at another home I visited. A lady who had not spoken for a long time was being visited by her daughter. When I entered the room and put Milo on the lady's lap, she said, 'Oh! Look at his face!' Her daughter couldn't believe it.

"Milo recently participated in a PAT-dog parade at Ely Cathedral, where a blessing of animals was being conducted. He loved every minute of it, and even managed to perform his own small miracle. There was a lady in a wheelchair present, with a condition that made her shake very badly. When I approached her,

Milo: An outgoing Yorkie who brightens the lives of everyone he visits.

she was shaking like a leaf, but, as soon as I put Milo on her lap, she stopped shaking and gave him a big cuddle. It's moments like these that make it all worthwhile.

"Of course, Yorkies are ideally suited to this type of work. Not only are their personalities just right, but their small size also means they are exactly the right size to be placed on an elderly person's lap.

"It's the same at schools. If a child is a little wary of dogs, Yorkies are ideal. Children are not intimidated by Yorkies because of their tiny size, and their cute faces mean most children find them irresistible."

CHAPTER EIGHT

SEEKING PERFECTION

The dog world has many beautiful and impressive breeds, but when it comes to glamor, the Yorkshire Terrier wins hands down. There is nothing more stunning than the sight of a Yorkshire Terrier, in full coat, moving across the show ring. The keen, alert expression is pure terrier, the brisk, purposeful gait tells you that this is a serious dog in a tiny frame, and the long, flowing coat is, quite simply, the icing on the cake.

As you may imagine, achieving this effect is not the work of a moment. The dedicated exhibitor spends many hours preparing a Yorkie for the ring, but, even more important is the work and dedication that goes into producing a top-quality animal that is sound in mind and body, and has all the true characteristics of the Yorkshire Terrier.

WHY SHOW YOUR DOG?

Showing is a wonderful hobby where you can meet lots of like-minded people, and enjoy a day out with your dog. But there is a serious side to

it. The majority of exhibitors are not showing their dogs simply to win a prize and gain the applause of the crowd. The aim is to get expert endorsement of the dog you are showing, and the kennel he represents. The judge has the crucial task of examining all the entries, and then deciding which dog, in his opinion, conforms most closely to the Breed Standard.

The Breed Standard is the written blueprint for the breed, which gives a detailed picture of what a Yorkshire Terrier should look like in terms of conformation, coat, and coloring, what his temperament should be, and how he should move. It is the bible for all breeders, and it is what keeps the Yorkshire Terrier looking as he was intended by the pioneers who developed the breed. If there were no written guidelines, it would be all too easy for little discrepancies to creep in, and, over a period of time, the true Yorkshire Terrier would be lost forever. It is for this reason that breeding and showing pedigree dogs is a serious undertaking, and should be given the diligence and dedication it deserves.

The Yorkie carries his head high, and has an air of importance.

muzzle should not be too long, and the nose should be black.

Eyes

The eyes are medium dark in color, sparkling, with a keen, intelligent expression. They should be positioned so that they look directly forward. The eye rims should be dark.

THE BREED STANDARD

The judge will use the Breed Standard of the show's governing authority, which, in most cases, will be that country's national kennel club. There are minor differences in the wording and terminology, depending on the Standard that is being used, but the overall picture is very much the same.

General appearance

A long-haired terrier, with a parting in the hair, which goes from nose to tail. The hair hangs down straight and falls evenly on either side. The Yorkshire Terrier is a compact, neat, well-proportioned dog. He carries his head held high, with a great air of self-importance.

Temperament

Alert and intelligent, the Yorkie has a spirited disposition.

Head

The head is small and rather flat on top. The

Ears

The ears are small and V-shaped. They are covered in short hair, which should be rich tan in color. The ears, which are carried erect, should not be set too far apart.

Mouth

The teeth should meet in a scissor bite, i.e., the upper teeth closely overlap the lower teeth.

Neck

There should be a good reach of neck. This stems back to the Yorkie's ratting past when he would have needed a good reach of neck in order to grab his quarry and shake it.

Forequarters

The legs should be straight when viewed from the front and from the side. They should be covered with hair that is a rich, golden tan. This can be slightly lighter at the ends than at the roots. The hair should not extend higher than the elbow. The shoulders should be well laid.

This means that, when viewed from the front, the shoulders should fit neatly into the side, with no obvious protrusion. The elbows should be close to the chest.

Body

The topline, which extends from the withers (the highest point of the dog) to the tail, should be level, and must remain level when the dog is moving. The body is compact, with a curved rib cage (known as a good spring of rib). The body should not appear flat or slab-sided. The loin (the area from the back of the rib cage to the pelvic bones) should be short and muscular.

Hindquarters

The legs should be straight when viewed from behind, and when the dog is moving they should drive with power. The upper thighs should be well muscled, and the stifle (the dog's knee) should have a moderate bend. The hocks (the joints on the hind legs below the second thigh) should be well angulated. The legs should be covered with rich, tan hair, which should not extend higher than the stifles. The hair may be a few shades lighter at the ends than at the roots.

Feet

The feet are round with black nails.

Tail

In the U.K. and the U.S., the tail is customarily docked to medium length. It is carried a little higher than the level of the back. The tail should be well covered with hair, which should be a darker blue than the rest of the body, especially at the end of the tail.

In the past, the tail was docked to one-third of its length, but now half the length is more common. Indeed, it seems tails are becoming longer, perhaps as the likelihood of a ban on docking increases. If this does happen, the tail set will become a vital issue. If the tail is set on slightly higher than the back, the dog will carry it upright, or curved over the back. If the tail is

The body is neat, compact, and well-proportioned.

low set, it will stream out behind the dog, and will ruin the compact, balanced outline that is typical of the breed.

Movement

The Yorkshire Terrier has a very distinctive action on the move. The dog should move freely, showing drive from behind. The action should appear straight from in front and from behind, and the topline should remain level. Despite being a small dog, the Yorkie should cover plenty of ground as he moves.

Coat

The Yorkie's coat is his crowning glory, and the Breed Standard goes into considerable detail as to the correct texture and color. The hair on the body should be long and straight, and it should feel fine and silky. A wavy coat is incorrect, and so is a coat that is either woolly or coarse. The hair on the head, known as the fall, should be long, and a rich, golden tan. It is deeper in color at the sides of the head, at the roots of the ears, and on the muzzle. The length of hair on the muzzle should be very long.

Color

The coat should be a dark, steel blue, and this should extend from the back of the skull to the root of the tail. The hair should not be so light as to be silver blue, and it should never be mingled with fawn, bronze, or dark hairs. The hair on the chest should be a rich tan, darker at the roots, becoming a little lighter in the middle, and at its lightest at the tips.

The purposeful, ground-covering gait of a typical Yorkie.

Weight

Both males and females should not exceed 7 pounds (3.2 kg) in weight. This weight stipulation should be seen as a guideline. In recent years, the tendency is for Yorkies to be slightly bigger, and, because of related health issues, this must be for the benefit of the breed. If a Yorkie conforms closely to the Breed Standard, most judges will not penalize a dog that is slightly over the stated weight limit.

BREEDING YORKIES

There are plenty of Yorkies in the world that cannot find homes, so do not rush into breeding a litter unless you have given the matter very serious consideration. Pet Yorkies are quite happy to go through their lives without being bred from, and there is no point in simply producing a litter of puppies without understanding what is truly involved. Unless you are amazingly lucky, you will produce nothing better than poor to average representatives of the breed. Breeding is a job for the experts, and this should be respected.

However, if you decide that you want to get seriously involved in breeding Yorkshire Terriers, you will find it a fascinating, if sometimes frustrating, undertaking. Where do you start? If you study the Breed Standard, and go to Championship/Specialty shows, where you will be able to see top-quality Yorkshire Terriers, you will have a fair idea of what the ideal Yorkie should look like. But how can you ensure that there will be a future Champion in the litter you breed?

The answer, in short, is that there is absolutely no guarantee. When it comes to breeding, the best-made plans can come unstuck, and you may be very disappointed with how your puppies develop. Equally, you may have a surprise, and a puppy may turn out better than you expected. If you accept the unpredictability of breeding pedigree dogs, you will be halfway to becoming successful! The other part of the equation comes down to minimizing the risk of failure, and this can be done by intensive research and planning.

The obvious, first step is to select a female that is worth breeding from. This may not always be a top-winning Yorkie, but it must be a dog that is typical of the breed, with no outstanding faults in coat, coloring, or conformation. She should have a good temperament, and she should be free from hereditary health problems (see Chapter Nine). In terms of breeding, a brood bitch must be big enough to be able to carry her puppies and to deliver them safely.

Before you decide to go ahead and breed from your bitch, you must research her

Success is sweet: Christine Crowther with her four home-bred Champions: Ch. Candytops Cassandra, Ch. Candytops Charmaine, Ch. Candytops Dream Lover, and Ch. Candytops Amelia Fair.

pedigree, and find out as much as possible about her family background. First, and most importantly, you need to check for inherited health problems, but then you need to find out what her parents, her grandparents, and, if possible, her great-grandparents look like. This will give you an idea of the strong points in your bitch's makeup, as well as the areas where she needs to improve.

It would be easy to mate your bitch to the top-winning Yorkie of the day, and hope that this would result in Champion offspring. Indeed, many newcomers to breeding make this mistake. However, it is far more important to find a male that will complement your bitch rather than going for the dog that is in fashion.

You need to look critically at a potential mate, and assess what are his best points. Even the best dog will have some minor faults, and you must evaluate these and check that they do not duplicate the weak areas in your bitch. You must then thoroughly research the male dog's pedigree, and find out as much as possible about the dogs in his background. As before, his relatives should be free from inherited health problems, and there should be no outstanding faults in the line.

The aim with every mating is to combine the best qualities of both male and female, and hopefully to eliminate as many faults as possible. You cannot hope that a major fault in one of the dogs will be corrected if the partner is strong in that area. Not all puppies may show the fault, but it will be in their makeup, and may come out if they are used for breeding. The aim is to match and complement male and female, cementing the good qualities, and trying to strengthen the weaker areas.

Breeders can choose from three types of breeding programs when they are planning a mating. The choice depends on what the breeder is hoping to achieve in the litter.

Inbreeding

This is the breeding of two very closely related dogs – for example, two dogs that have the same sire (father). This type of breeding can be used when you want to accentuate – very quickly – a particular trait associated with that family.

Inbreeding should not be attempted by the novice. It requires the skill of an experienced breeder who knows the detailed histories of the dogs involved, and who will only proceed if they are confident that the resulting offspring will be sound and healthy, as well as being typical specimens of the breed.

Linebreeding

This is similar to inbreeding in that it involves mating members of the same family, but they are not so closely related. This is the most commonly used breeding program, as it retains the virtues of a line, but it also introduces new blood.

Outcrossing

This is the mating of totally unrelated dogs that have no relatives in common. It is a method of introducing completely new blood to a line, and if you produce the result you are looking for, you can fix the type by linebreeding.

ASSESSING THE LITTER

Once your litter has been born, the next task is to select the puppy that has the potential of becoming a Champion. Some breeders claim they can evaluate a puppy at the moment of birth (when it is still wet), but others are more circumspect, and prefer to wait a little longer before picking out the star of the litter.

When a puppy is around 12–16 weeks, an experienced breeder will have a fair idea of how

Inbreeding

The Patajohn kennel, owned by Pat and John Allington, has an international reputation, but luck can still play a part in the best-run establishments.

Two of the Patajohn Champions, Magic and Mysterious, decided to take matters into their own hands, and an accidental mating took place. The result was a wonderful litter, which included an Australian Champion.

"Because the litter was so good, we decided to repeat the mating," said Pat. "This time we got two Champions in the litter: Ch. Patajohn Rebel and Ch. Patajohn Perhaps. I think the secret is to study the pedigrees very carefully, and see if the dogs can stand up to close interbreeding."

Ch. Patajohn Rebel.

Parents	Grandparents	Great-Grandparents	Great-Great-Grandparents
Ch. Patajohn Magic	Ch. Crosspins Royal Brigadier	Crosspins Gaye Chance	Bradstara Royalist
			Finstal Victoria
		Crosspins Midnight Rose	Bradstara Royalist
			Crosspins Reckless Imp
	Patajohn Merry Go Round	Ch. Brybett Finesse	Brybett Dedication
			Brybett Brambles Wish
		Patajohn Petals Dream	Patajohn Extra Special
			Patajohn Stephanie
Ch. Patajohn Mysterious	Ch. Patajohn Magic	Ch. Crosspins Royal Brigadier	Crosspins Gaye Chance
			Crosspins Midnight Rose
		Patajohn Merry Go Round	Ch. Brybett Finesse
			Patajohn Petals Dream
	Patajohn Puddles Love	Ch. Ozmilion Admiration	Ch. Ozmilion Invitation
			Ch. Ozmilion Lone Romance
		Patajohn Uptown Girl	Chandas Little Charmer
			Patajohn Jayne

Linebreeding

Wendy White-Thomas has made up eight Champions under her Wenwytes affix, including the linebred Ch. Wenwytes Wild Intrigue.

"I used a bitch that I had bred but never shown, called Wenwytes Whiskey's Trail," said Wendy. "I put her to Ch. Wenwytes Whisky's Boy, with the aim of improving color and tail placement. I was delighted with the litter, and Ch. Wenwytes Wild Intrigue is very strong in the two areas where I was seeking to find improvement."

Ch. Wenwytes Wild Intrigue: Improving on existing lines.

Parents	Grandparents	Great-Grandparents	Great-Great-Grandparents
Ch. Wenwytes Whisky's Boy	Wenwytes Whisky Magic	Ch. Patajohn Magic	Ch. Crosspins Royal Brigadier
			Patajohn Merry Go Round
		Ch. Wenwytes Whisky Galore	Herbies Whisky Mac
			Wenwytes Well To Do
	Wenwytes Way Ahead	Ch. Chevawn Special Engagement at Wenwytes	Chevawn Special Charmer
			Sharisel Missy's Madam Chevawn
		Wenwytes Well To Do	Ch. Finstal Johnathan
			Wenwytes Bright Future
Wenwytes Whisky's Trail	Ch. Wenwytes Without Question	Ch. Wenwytes Without Doubt	Ch. Wenwytes Whispers Boy
			Welcome Magic At Wenwytes
		Yorlang Yasmin	Ch. Chevawn Special Engagement at Wenwytes
			Yorlang Additional Class
	Wenwytes Whisky Galore	Herbies Whisky Mac	Herbies Perry Champers
			Wenwytes Welcome Angel
		Wenwytes Well To Do	Ch. Finstal Johnathan
			Wenwytes Bright Future

Outcrossing

Christine Crowther has been breeding Yorkshire Terriers since the late 1960s, and her Candytops kennel has enjoyed a huge amount of success in the ring. She has worked intensively on her own breeding program, but, like all lines, there is a periodical need to bring in fresh blood.

"I used my own bitch, Candytops She's a Lady, and I mated her to Ch. Crosspins Royal Brigadier, who is a complete outcross," said Christine. "I liked everything about him: his outline, his color, and his head, and I thought I would get a good result if I used a bitch that was very strongly linebred." The result was Candytops Dream Lover, who gained her title in 1996 and was top-winning bitch.

Ch. Candytops Dream Lover: A carefully planned outcross.

Parents	Grandparents	Great-Grandparents	Great-Great-Grandparents
Ch. Crosspins Royal Brigadier	Ch. Crosspins Gaye Chance	Bradstara Royalist	Blairsville Royal Monarch
			Bradstara Tina
		Finstal Victoria	Garsims Captain Moonshine
			Ringlet Of Finstal
	Crosspins Midnight Rose	Bradstara Royalist	Blairsville Royal Monarch
			Bradstara Tina
		Crosspins Reckless Imph	Bradstara Royalist
			Barntoys Honey Suckle Rose
Candytops She's A Lady	Ch. Candytops Royal Sovereign	Ch. Candytops Royal Cascade	Ch. Candytops Cavalcadia
			Candytops Ribbons Delight
		Candytops Lady Levant	Ch. Candytops Cavalcadia
			Candytops So Fare
	Candytops Royal Fergie	Ch. Candytops Royal Cascade	Ch. Candytops Cavalcadia
			Candytops Ribbons Delight
		Candytops Sue Ellen	Ch. Candytops Candyman
			Sophie Of Candytops

An experienced breeder will be able to evaluate the finer points of a young puppy.

he will mature. Ideally, a breeder would hold on to a dog until six months, or even older, before making a final decision.

To begin with, a breeder would evaluate a puppy by standing him in a show pose in order to assess conformation. The body should appear neat and compact, with a level back. The legs should be straight, and the shoulders should fit neatly into the sides. The tail should be set slightly higher than the level of the back.

Dentition can be a problem in the breed, so the mouth should be examined carefully. Even when the milk teeth are still present, it is possible to tell if a puppy has the correct scissor bite, where the top teeth closely overlap the bottom teeth. Generally, it seems that dentition is more likely to be correct in a puppy that has a slightly wider jaw. If a puppy has a narrow, pinched jaw, he may well suffer from over-crowding when the adult teeth come through.

The coat looks very different from the adult version, but there are a number of telltale features. Beware the coat that is jet black and red; it is unlikely that these extremes of color will develop into the correct shades of steel blue and rich, golden tan. It is safer to go for a mid-range of color, for example, a blue-black coat will probably become a good steel blue in maturity. If the coat is brown-black, it rarely becomes the correct color. A good indication of final coat color is to look at the color of the puppy's skin. If he has blue skin, he will probably develop the correct steel blue coat; if the skin is pink, the coat may well end up too light.

The tan coat may appear fairly light and still become a rich, golden tan, as long as there is some evidence of this shade on the coat, such as on the muzzle or on the feet. A tan can appear quite creamy at this age, and still develop correctly.

Although the puppy has a short coat, you can still assess texture. The puppy coat should be straight and quite profuse. The development of the coat depends on the bloodlines, and the rate of growth and the progression of the shades may vary considerably. A puppy may appear to have quite a thin coat, and then it will suddenly burst through. Avoid a coat that is hard and spiky, with a harsh texture. This puppy will make a nice pet, but he will never develop the silky coat that is typical of the Yorkie. The other coat to avoid is the woolly type, which is often very profuse. Again, this coat will never develop correctly, and it often has to be clipped quite severely in order to keep it in reasonable order.

It is always a good plan to see the parents of a puppy, and, if possible, any other close relatives, as this will give you the best indication of how the coat is likely to turn out.

Finally, the breeder will assess a puppy on the move. This will give clues as to whether the puppy has the correct conformation, and if he has the vigorous, driving action that is asked for in the Breed Standard.

Wendy White-Thomas has kept Yorkshire Terriers for more than 30 years, and her Wenwytes kennel has a reputation for producing sound Yorkies of impeccable quality. She has made up a total of eight British Champions, and is currently campaigning Ch. Wenwytes Wild Intrigue – one of the youngest Yorkies ever to gain his title.

"I am a farmer's daughter and I have owned dogs all my life," said Wendy. "But it was not until after I was married and had my own home that I decided that the Yorkshire Terrier was the breed for me. I had previously shown horses, but, with two small children, I found it impossible to continue. My aunt had a Yorkie, and that was my introduction to the breed. I knew right away that I wanted to own Yorkshire Terriers and show them, and I have been involved with the breed ever since.

Wendy with Ch. Wenwytes Wild Dancer.

"My first Yorkie of real quality was Crystal Clear At Wenwytes, who I bought from Mrs. Beach of the Beachdale kennel. At this stage, I was not ready to start showing, but I went to all the shows and watched everything that was going on in the ring. I looked at the different types of Yorkshire Terriers and the way they were handled. My experience with horses proved to be valuable, as I already had an eye for conformation and movement, which I was able to use when I was looking at Yorkies. There was one dog that I always looked out for – Ch. Blairsville Royal Seal, owned by Brian Lister, who became the breed recordholder with

50 CCs, all awarded under different judges. I always said to myself: 'If I could breed a dog like that, then I really would be getting somewhere.'

"It has taken many years, but I would say that Monty (Ch. Wenwytes Wild Intrigue) has something of Royal Seal in him." To date, Monty (pictured on page 104), who is only two years old, has won five CCs, including a Group 3 placing in the Toy Group.

There is no denying that the Yorkie's coat is of major significance in the show ring. But Wendy believes it should never disguise the dog that is underneath. "There is no point in putting icing on a second-rate cake," she said. "A dog has to be made right and move correctly before you start worrying about the coat."

Spotting a show prospect is never easy, but in Yorkshire Terriers, where the coat changes so dramatically, it is even more difficult. However, Wendy sticks to her principles and looks at the way a puppy is put together. "A puppy should be a miniature of the adult, obviously minus the coat," she said. "I like to see a reasonable length of neck, a nice, level topline, and a good tail set. I see too many dogs in the ring with a low tail set, and when the time comes when we cannot dock, this type of dog will look completely unbalanced." Wendy also likes a pup that has attitude. "I like to see a certain presence – a feeling of 'look at me.' This type of dog is going to enjoy showing, and will always give his best."

It is also important to evaluate a puppy's temperament. In order to show himself to his full potential, a dog must have an air of showmanship. He should be the type that thrives on being in the limelight, and is not daunted by big crowds. If a dog enjoys his showing, he will give his best. If he hates the whole business, he will look cowed and miserable, and it is better to leave him at home.

SHOW TRAINING

As well as giving a show puppy basic training and socialization, you also need to teach him how to behave in the ring. It sounds simple enough to stand in show pose, to be examined by a judge, and to move in the ring, but it is important to remember that the show ring is a very challenging environment. There will be lots of noise, such as loudspeaker announcements and the applause from other rings, there will be crowds of people, and there will be numerous dogs to distract your Yorkie from the job at hand.

The best way to prepare your Yorkie for the ring is to take him to training classes that specialize in show training. Your Yorkie will get used to concentrating on you, even though there are other dogs around, and he will get used to being examined by strangers. In the ring, the judge will make a thorough examination of each dog, looking at the teeth, running his hands over the body to assess the conformation, brushing the coat, and, in the case of males, checking for the presence of testicles. This is a major invasion of a dog's personal space, but a show dog must

learn to accept this type of handling without resentment.

The secret is to accustom your puppy to being handled from an early age, and be ready to reward him with a treat when he cooperates. When your puppy is used to being handled by you, ask friends and family members to examine him. By the time you get to training classes, your Yorkie will be quite happy with this aspect of showing.

The show pose

By tradition, in the U.K. the Yorkshire Terrier is shown on a red box, and there is no doubt that this sets off his long coat to perfection. In the U.S., he is shown on a table. A Yorkie that is used to being groomed on the table will have no problem with standing on a box/table, but again, it is a good idea to work at this aspect of training from an early age.

To begin with, reward your puppy for just standing on the box/table for a few seconds. If he is rewarded when he is actually on the box, he will start to associate it with good things, and he will always be willing to be lifted on to his box/table.

In the U.K., the lead is held above the dog's head, and the Yorkie maintains his own pose, standing in profile with his head head high, and his body still. In the U.S., the exhibitor will usually also hold the tail in place. In both cases, you should allow the dog to show himself, and not string him up by his lead.

When you are training, gradually increase the length of time your dog maintains his pose before rewarding. Some exhibitors always use a food reward, choosing something especially tasty, such as cheese or chicken. Other exhibitors use a favorite toy, and a Yorkie will look eager and interested as he looks at the toy, and can then be rewarded as soon as the judge has moved on.

Moving your Yorkie

The judge will want to see each Yorkshire Terrier move. Generally, the exhibitor will be asked to move the dog so that the judge can assess movement from the front, from the rear, and from the side. This can be make or break time, as a Yorkie moving forward in a happy, purposeful manner, with his coat flowing, gives a wonderful impression. The reluctant show dog that looks miserable and drags on the lead will not show himself to his advantage.

Work at this aspect of show training, using a toy or a treat to encourage your dog to move forward. Do not keep fussing, or he will quickly become bored. Inevitably, you will brush the coat in place, and just as you start moving, your Yorkie will decide to have a good shake! If this happens, do not panic. Stop, give the coat a quick brush if it is badly out of place, and then continue on your way. Remember to be happy and positive in your manner, as feelings are very quickly transmitted down the lead.

PREPARING FOR A SHOW

Show training is an ongoing business, particularly when Yorkies are maturing. If your Yorkie starts to rebel against being shown,

The well-trained show dog learns to pose for the judge.

particularly during adolescence, it is better to put showing to one side for a few months. Allow him the chance to find his feet in the world before putting him under any more pressure. There are some Yorkies who seem to be natural showmen, and come into their own as they step into the ring. These dogs are a real gift, and you should enjoy every minute of their showing career.

Assuming that your Yorkie is mentally and physically fit for competition, you must now get to work on his coat to ensure that it is looking its very best on the day of the show. Obviously, your Yorkie will have his coat in papers, and so it is a matter of planning the coat care, depending on how far you have to travel to the show.

If you have a long journey, you will need to bathe your dog the evening before the show. If you have sufficient time, you can leave the bath until the morning.

• Before bathing, you will need to go through your regular routine of checking eyes and ears, and cleaning if necessary. The nails may also need to be trimmed.

GOLDEN DAYS

Cher Hildebrand of Goldenray Yorkies, Dayton, Ohio, started going to shows as a spectator, but she soon got bitten by the showing bug…

"I was attracted to Yorkies firstly for their beauty, and secondly for their attitudes. They are outgoing, friendly, and affectionate dogs, but they hold on to their independence, which suits my personality ideally.

"Once I decided I wanted a Yorkie, I bought a few breed books and decided that showing sounded like a hobby I would enjoy. After that, I read everything I could find on the subject, as well as subscribing to every breed magazine. I have never regretted my decision, although there are times when I think I must be a little crazy to enjoy the sport so much!

"To begin with, I went to shows as a spectator only, to get an idea of what was involved. After that, I entered with a Pomeranian and amazed myself by winning, although I think that was partly due to the fact that I had a mentor guiding me through the process, telling me when to enter the ring. I'd advise anyone thinking of taking up showing to find someone more experienced, preferably a really good Yorkie breeder, who can guide them through their first few shows. It's a really big help.

"I've had some funny moments handling my Yorkies in the show ring. On one occasion,

Cher showing Ch. Goldenray Juvenile Delinquent.

when my dog got placed by the judge, I went to go forward and the dog's lead got caught in one of my hoop earrings. It took me ages to free it, by which time the judge was coming forward to offer his help! Fortunately, none of this affected my dog's placing, but, needless to say, I don't wear hoop earrings when I am showing anymore.

"I show my own Yorkies and have always preferred to do this rather than employ a professional handler. However, I have had times in the past where I have been unable to show my dogs and I've had to use a handler.

"Generally, I think it is better to show your dogs yourself, but, for a variety of reasons, many people cannot and a good handler more than fills that gap.

"My most exciting win has got to be the year I won the Yorkshire Terrier Club of America New York Specialty show with Ch. Goldenray New Year Hope. Winning at a Specialty show is a major achievement, as it takes a great deal of effort and commitment, not to mention the fact that the serious competitors attend shows nearly every weekend!

"As I breed my own dogs, showing is important to my kennels. But every dog I breed is produced as a companion first and a show dog second, but I can't describe the joy and satisfaction you get if you finish a title on a dog you have bred yourself."

- Brush the coat, and decide if any trimming is required. You may need to trim around the ears, around the feet, and between the pads. Brush the coat to its full length, and decide if it is the correct length. Ideally, it should fall to the ground, and then be about one inch (2.5 cm) longer than the height of your Yorkshire Terrier.
- Put the coat back into papers, but do not apply oil.
- When you get to the showground, give your Yorkie a chance to stretch his legs, and then set up your grooming table.
- Take out the papers, and then brush and comb through the coat. You will need to spray the coat with water to get rid of any wrinkles.
- Tie the topknot in a bow (in the U.S., the top-knot may be divided and tied with two bows)

Give your Yorkie the chance to move freely.

and then you will be ready to go!

- It is advisable to allow at least one hour to get your Yorkshire Terrier ready once you arrive at the showground.

SPORTSMANSHIP

Showing is a great hobby, particularly when you are winning! However, there are days when things just do not go your way, or it may be that the judge has a preference for a different type of Yorkie to the one you are showing.

When it all comes down to it, you are reliant on the personal opinion of the judge, and so, inevitably, showing is full of highs and lows.

Enjoy your wins, but, just as importantly, be gracious when you lose, and be the first to go and congratulate the winning team. Remember, regardless of the outcome of the judging, you are the most fortunate person at the show, because you are taking your beloved Yorkie home with you.

CHAPTER NINE

HEALTH CARE

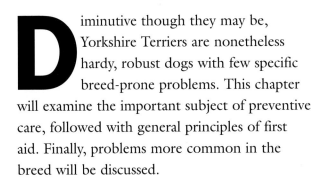

Diminutive though they may be, Yorkshire Terriers are nonetheless hardy, robust dogs with few specific breed-prone problems. This chapter will examine the important subject of preventive care, followed with general principles of first aid. Finally, problems more common in the breed will be discussed.

PREVENTIVE CARE

Responsible preventive care involves:
• A vaccination program tailored to suit the needs of your dog, your lifestyle, and your environment.
• Comprehensive parasite control.
• Adequate exercise, tailored to your dog's age and needs. Yorkies are robust little terriers and will happily match your pace and endurance.
• Regular grooming and health checks (see Chapter Six).

VACCINATION

Vaccination or inoculation (and throughout this chapter the terms will be used synonymously) stimulates the dog to produce active immunity against one or more diseases without developing any symptoms of that disease. This is despite the fact that the causative organism has been introduced into the body. This is achieved by altering the causative bacteria or viruses (pathogens) so that they cannot produce disease. The alteration does not interfere with the dog's immune system's ability to recognize the pathogen as a threat and build up protection in the form of antibodies. The pathogens can be killed (inactivated) or weakened (attenuated) to render them safe.

Once altered, the appropriate pathogens can be introduced into the body by various routes. For example, vaccination against kennel cough (infectious bronchotracheitis) is by the administration of nasal drops. Inoculations generally involve injections, perhaps one of the reasons that these are so often referred to as "jabs."

Regardless of whether the vaccine is inactivated or attenuated, the body responds with active immunity. Immunity lasts a variable time, depending on factors such as the vaccine, disease, age, and the dog's state of health.

Puppies acquire natural immunity from their mother.

Puppies

Are puppies born with immunity? Puppies are usually born with some immunity that is acquired from their dam while they are still in the womb. The necessary antibodies are carried in the blood and cross the placenta into the puppy. This is called acquired or passive immunity. It lasts for only about three weeks if not regularly topped up via antibodies absorbed from the milk when nursing.

Passive protection starts to wane once weaning begins. It disappears about a month after the puppy has left the dam. This is the correct time to start vaccinations. It is also the danger period for the puppy since, at this time, he is susceptible to any naturally acquired infection. It is for this reason you are asked to isolate your Yorkie puppy for 10-14 days after completion of inoculation, while active immunity develops to the vaccine. During this period, the puppy is still vulnerable, even though the inoculation has been given.

One of the aims of vaccine manufacturers is to develop vaccines that will confer solid protection in the shortest possible time, even when circulating maternal antibodies are present. Canine vaccines are now available that will give protection by 10-12 weeks of age. This affords your puppy early immunity and allows early socialization and training. Let your new puppy get over the stress of his new surroundings for a day or two, and then contact your veterinarian for an appointment.

Boosters

Vaccination does not give lifelong immunity. Reinforcement (boosting) will be required. Killed vaccines generally require more frequent boosting, usually annually, although sometimes even less.

Today most canine vaccines are multivalent, i.e., they cover several diseases with one injection. Short-acting (usually inactivated) components are often incorporated into the multidisease vaccine. The time of re-inoculation (boosting) of the product as a whole is based on the component that gives the shortest protection. Although protection against distemper and hepatitis will last much longer than a year, when this is combined with leptospirosis, the manufacturer's recommendation will be that an annual booster of the combined vaccine is advised.

Vaccination reactions

Until relatively recently, the use of vaccines has entirely depended on manufacturers' recommendations. In response to owners' concerns regarding possible vaccination reactions, this is altering. It is now advised that primary vaccination and boosters are tailored for individual requirements. Discuss this with your veterinarian at the time of your puppy's first visit.

In a very small number of cases, there is evidence that vaccinations can result in unexpected reactions. These usually involve the immune system, and result in problems such as anemia. Vaccines should be assessed in terms of risks and benefits. My view is that risk exists, but the risk of re-emergence of these killer diseases is much greater if we allow our pets' immune status to fall dangerously low.

A dog's resistance to a variety of diseases can be determined from a small blood sample. This will indicate whether boosting is required for any particular disease. The benefit is that unnecessary inoculation is avoided,

but the disadvantage is that such a procedure will be considerably more expensive than a combined booster injection. Stress for the dog also has to be considered. Yorkshire Terriers can be feisty about venipuncture. A simple sub-cutaneous jab is much more to their taste.

If you have concerns, discuss them with your veterinarian and reach an informed decision.

Core and noncore vaccines

Core vaccines are the necessary ones that protect against diseases that are serious, fatal, or difficult to treat. In Britain, these include distemper, parvovirus, and hepatitis (adenovirus) disease.

Your veterinarian will advise you when to start the vaccination program.

In North America, rabies is also a core vaccine. In the U.K. this is only the case if you intend to travel to any of the countries in the PETS scheme. This allows entry into Britain without having to undergo the mandatory six months' quarantine.

Noncore vaccines include bordetella (kennel cough) and leptospirosis (kidney disease). In the U.S., other diseases, such as coronovirus (which causes diarrhea) and borellia (Lyme disease, which causes infective polyarthritis), are included. The noncore vaccines that are used depend upon a risk assessment with your veterinarian.

Informed veterinary opinion is that primary inoculation and the first annual booster when the puppy is about 15 months of age, are sound, preventive medicine. These should include both core vaccines and those noncore vaccines considered appropriate.

Future vaccinations, and their frequency, will then depend upon such factors as local infection levels, breed susceptibilities, and your Yorkshire Terrier's lifestyle (for example, if he is regularly attending shows, training classes, boarding kennels, etc.).

Canine Distemper

Canine distemper is no longer widespread in most developed Western countries, solely due to vaccination.

The signs (symptoms) of distemper include fever, diarrhea, coughing, with discharges from the nose and eyes. With the "Hardpad" variant, the pads harden. A significant proportion of infected dogs develop nervous signs, including fits, chorea (twitching muscles), and paralysis.

Due to vaccination, distemper is hardly ever seen in Britain today. Do not be misled! The virus is still out there, waiting for its opportunity. This was demonstrated in Finland only a few years ago, when a serious epidemic of distemper occurred solely due to falling levels of immunity in the canine population.

Hepatitis

Also known as adenovirus disease, signs range from sudden death in peracute infection, to mild cases where the dog only appears to be a bit "off color." In severe cases, there is usually fever, enlargement of all the lymph nodes (glands), and a swollen liver. Sometimes "blue eye" can occur. The eyes look opaque and bluish due to the swelling of the cornea (the clear part of the eye). Fortunately, the condition usually resolves quickly without problems.

Parvovirus

This virus is very stable and can survive in the environment for a long time. The disease reached epidemic proportions in Europe and North America in the 1980s. Signs include vomiting and blood-stained diarrhea (dysentery).

The rapid development of safe, effective vaccines brought the disease under control in the Western world, although it is still a serious killer, rivaling only that of distemper in many other countries.

Rabies

Rabies vaccination is compulsory in many countries, including the United States. In Britain, it is mandatory for dogs traveling under the PETS scheme. The virus is spread by bites from infected animals. These include foxes in Europe, and stray dogs in other parts of the world.

Kennel Cough

This syndrome (collection of signs) is considered to be due to several pathogens, including parainfluenza viruses and bordetella bacteria.

In North America, parainfluenza is considered to be the primary cause, whereas in Britain, bacterial bordetella is considered the culprit. Distemper and adenoviruses also play a part in some cases.

Regardless of the cause, the disease is not usually life-threatening, except in very young and very old dogs. A persistent cough for three to four weeks is the main symptom, which results in rapid spread of the disease.

1. Parainfluenza vaccination
A parainfluenza component has been incorporated in multivalent vaccines for several years. Manufacturers recommend annual re-vaccination, but in high-risk situations, e.g., boarding kennels, shows, etc., more frequent revaccination is advised.

2. Bordetellosis vaccination
Unlike parainfluenza, bordetella is not

Vaccination against rabies is compulsory in the United States.

incorporated into the usual multivalent vaccines, since it is usually administered separately, via nasal drops. This is because nasal drops have been demonstrated to give better immunity than conventional inoculation methods, such as injection.

In Britain, there is a combined parainfluenza and bordetella intranasal vaccine available. If you go to shows, training classes, or regularly board your Yorkshire Terrier, think about protection against bordetellosis and parainfluenza.

Yorkies can suffer from narrowed airway problems (tracheal collapse) when any respiratory infection will cause serious breathing difficulties (see page 127). Prevention is better than cure!

Leptospirosis

Leptospirosis is caused by bacteria and not viruses. Protection against two diseases is currently provided by the killed (inactivated) leptospirosis vaccine.

Leptospira canicola is spread mainly in the urine of infected dogs. *Leptospira icterohaemorrhagiae* is spread by rats. Both types cause disease in dogs and can spread to humans.

Recent work has shown that dogs infected with leptospirosis in the U.K. and in the U.S. are usually infected with other types. The reason for the present vaccination is based on the zoonotic potential of the contained leptospiral organisms (i.e., its ability to transfer to humans). The leptospirosis vaccine is probably the shortest acting of all the various components in multivalent vaccines.

Canine coronavirus

This virus can cause diarrhea, particularly in puppies. The disease is usually mild, and responds to supportive therapy. A vaccine is available in North America and some European countries, but no licensed vaccine is currently available in Britain.

Lyme disease (Borreliosis)

This disease is carried by certain ticks whose bite can transmit the disease to dogs and man. It is very common in parts of North America, and it does occur in Britain. It causes acute polyarthritis in both dogs and people. Fever, and heart, kidney, and neurological problems can also occur.

Although vaccines are available in North America, there is currently no licensed vaccine available in Britain.

PARASITES

Parasite control is an important part of preventive health care and is essential for all dogs, regardless of size or lifestyle. Parasites can be divided into two groups:
1. Ectoparasites live on the surface of the host and include fleas, lice, ticks, and mites.
2. Endoparasites live within the host. Worms are the best known, although other important endoparasites will be discussed.

ECTOPARASITES
Fleas

Fleas are the most common ectoparasites found on dogs. They are found worldwide. Yorkshire Terriers may be Toy dogs, but they have a hunting heritage and enjoy the great outdoors. Fleas can be picked up from the environment, or from contact with other animals.

Some dogs can carry a very high flea burden without problem, whereas others will show evidence of typical flea allergy dermatitis (FAD). FAD is not uncommon in the breed, and often develops due to chronic contact with fleas. Fleas are not host-specific. Often the pet cat is the culprit. Once hypersensitivity occurs, all that is needed is a bite from one flea to start serious pruritis (itching). Sometimes no fleas can be found on the dog, although there is usually evidence of flea dirt. Always check for these when grooming. Cat fleas can affect

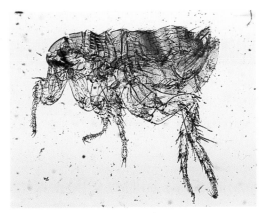

The dog flea – Ctenocephalides canis.

a range of other animals, including ourselves and our dogs.

Effective control involves both adult fleas on the animal, and the immature stages, which develop in the home. Fleas need a meal of blood to complete their life cycle. The adult flea then lays eggs on the host. These eggs soon drop to the ground. Provided temperature and humidity are suitable, they develop into larvae (immature forms) in carpets or gaps between floorboards.

Development can also take place outdoors, if conditions are suitable, as occurs in many of the southern states of the U.S. and could happen in Britain with increasingly warm and humid summers. Many pet dogs and cats have areas, even in tiny town yards, where they like to lie. Such areas can be difficult to render flea free!

Under ideal conditions, the life cycle can be completed in only three weeks. Sometimes, fleas can live without feeding for more than a year. This is why dogs and people can be bitten when entering a property that has been left unoccupied for some time.

Flea control

Adult fleas account for only approximately 5 percent of the total flea population. Control of the other 95 percent, consisting of immature stages, can be much more difficult. Few environmental insecticides have any effect against immature fleas, so an insecticide with prolonged action should be used. This will be effective against any subsequently emerging adults. Control in the home should also involve thorough vacuuming to remove any flea larvae.

Oral preparations are available, which, given to your dog, will prevent the completion of the flea's life cycle. The compound is transferred to the adult flea when it bites the dog for the all-essential blood meal.

There are many effective preparations to control adult fleas on the dog. Sprays can be used, but most dogs dislike the noise and care must be taken to avoid the eyes. Powders are effective but messy to use, and they have a very limited effect. Insecticidal baths are useful for killing adult fleas in the coat, but they do not have a lasting effect. Bathing should always be combined with other methods of flea control to prevent rapid reinfestation.

Prolonged action spot-on preparations are very effective and are easy to use on a lively Yorkie. These preparations contain chemicals that are lethal to the flea. They are dissolved in a substance that spreads through the invisible fat layer on the skin. Within 24 hours, the dog has total protection against fleas for approximately two months.

Yorkies that live in the country are more likely to pick up ticks.

When the flea bites your pet for that all-essential blood meal, it has to penetrate the fat layer to get to the blood supply, and, by so doing, ingests the ectoparasiticide. If the animal gets wet or is bathed occasionally, the treatment is not affected.

It is important to reapply the preparation according to the manufacturers' recommendations. This is usually every 30 or 60 days depending on the product. Some preparations are also effective against certain endoparasites, particularly roundworms. These are called endectocides.

Lice

Lice can sometimes be a problem in young Yorkshire Terriers. Unlike fleas, lice require direct contact for transmission, and the whole life cycle occurs on the host. The eggs (nits) are attached to individual hairs. Infestation is usually associated with violent irritation, and often affects the head and ears.

Unlike fleas, lice can be controlled by bathing in an effective ectoparasite shampoo.

Ticks

Ticks are carriers of various diseases. Lyme disease (borelliosis), babesiosis, and ehrlichiosis are examples. Although these diseases have been recognized in the U.K., they are more common in warmer parts of Europe and the United States.

Several flea and lice preparations are effective for tick control. Your veterinarian will advise on the best choice.

Cheyletiellosis

Cheyletiella yasguri, the causal mite for a condition called "walking dandruff," can just be seen by the naked eye as a tiny, white speck; hence the term. Young Yorkshire Terriers appearing itchy and scaly, particularly along the back, are prime suspects.

The mite is zoonotic and can cause intense irritation, particularly in children. Adult dogs, often showing no signs, act as carriers in kennels. Sprays, bathing, and spot-on preparations are all effective. Other pets should be treated to ensure that reinfestation does not recur. Veterinary advice should be sought.

Harvest mites

These are the larvae (immature forms) of a mite that lives in decaying organic matter. Also known as "chiggers" or "redbugs," they are red in color and just visible to the naked eye. Yorkies, particularly if exercised in fields and woodlands with a chalky soil, can become infested. Feet, muzzle, and head are target areas. Intense irritation results.

Any of the usual insecticidal sprays or washes are effective, but reapplication is necessary if you live in an area where this larval mite is common.

Mange

Mange is a parasitic skin disease caused by microscopic mites. Three types of mange can occur in the Yorkshire Terrier.

1. Demodectic mange

Demodex mites live in the hair follicles and sebaceous glands of many normal dogs. They only cause problems if the dog is immuno-incompetent, when the mite will start to multiply. Therefore, the condition is not as contagious as the other types of mange. In multidog households, often only one dog will be affected. Signs include inflammation and hair loss. Itching is often minimal but secondary bacterial infection can be a problem.

Veterinary treatment using modern preparations is effective once a positive diagnosis has been made. However, the implication of an underlying immune problem means that affected dogs should not be bred.

2. Otodectic mange

Ear mite infestation (otocariasis) is not that uncommon in the Yorkshire Terriers, particularly

All puppies need to be treated for roundworm.

if the home is shared with a cat. Adult cats often carry large numbers of the causal mite, *Otodectes cyanotis*, without showing symptoms. Signs include head shaking and scratching, often with a brown, smelly discharge from the ear. Consult your veterinarian for treatment and prevention advice, which must include in-contact animals.

3. Sarcoptic mange

Sarcoptic mange (scabies) affects many animals, including humans. Children are particularly susceptible and can develop intensely itchy areas on the arms and abdomen as a result of nursing the affected animal.

Modern treatments are effective but depend on accurate diagnosis, which sometimes requires repeated skin scrapings. Consult your veterinarian.

ENDOPARASITES

Intestinal worms are by far the most important endoparasites in the dog. Protozoan parasites, such as coccidia and giardia, may also be a problem in certain areas, together with blood-borne parasites, such as babesia.

Roundworms or nematodes

Until relatively recently, puppies were always wormy. The development of effective roundworm remedies and understanding of the complex life cycle has now resulted in a dramatic reduction of the problem.

The most common roundworm is *Toxacara canis*. This is a large, round, white worm 3-6 inches (7-15 cm) long. The life cycle is complex. Puppies can be born with toxocariasis acquired from their mother before birth. Regular worming of puppies and adults is essential.

Roundworm larvae can remain dormant in the tissues of adult dogs indefinitely. In bitches, under the influence of hormones during pregnancy, they become activated, cross the placenta in the bloodstream, and enter the puppies. They finally develop into adult worms in the small intestine. Larvae can also be passed from the bitch to the puppy during suckling.

There are now many safe and effective worm treatments available. Endectocides are spot-on preparations similar to those used for flea control. They contain drugs (e.g., selamectin) that are effective against roundworms, heartworms, and also fleas. Endectocides can be useful if you have difficulty administering oral preparations.

There are preparations licensed for use in puppies from as early as 14 days of age. Some are available "over the counter," but veterinary help is worthwhile to establish an effective lifelong worming strategy.

There is a slight risk of roundworms being transmitted to humans. For this reason, veterinarians advise that all adult dogs are routinely wormed approximately twice a year.

Tapeworms or cestodes

These are the other common intestinal worms found in the dog. Unlike roundworms, they do not have a direct life cycle, so spread is not from dog to dog but has to be through an intermediate host. This varies according to the type of tapeworm and includes fleas, sheep, horses, rodents, and sometimes even us!

In the dog, the most common type of tapeworm is *Dipylidium caninum*. This worm, which can be up to 20 inches (50 cm), uses the flea as the intermediate host.

The worms live in the intestine. Eggs contained within mature segments are shed from the end of the worm and pass out in the dog's feces. These segments are sticky and look like small grains of rice. In infested dogs they can often be seen around the anus. The segments finally fall to the ground, and burst, releasing the microscopic eggs.

Free-living flea larvae eat these fertilized eggs, which develop as the flea matures. When the adult flea is swallowed by a susceptible dog, the life cycle of the tapeworm is completed.

Effective treatment involves the tapeworm and eradication of fleas in the environment. Enlist the help of your veterinarian.

Echinococcus

Echinococcus species are important because of their zoonotic potential. *Echinococcus multilocularis* can cause serious cysts in the lungs of people. Under the PETS scheme, dogs and cats have to be treated with specific remedies against this cestode (and be certified) before entry or reentry is allowed. This should be borne in mind if you intend to travel to any of the PETS-authorized countries from Britain with your Yorkie.

Other tapeworms can occasionally be a problem in outdoor-loving Yorkies that regularly hunt or scavenge, eating the meat of intermediate hosts such as rats, rabbits, and similar wildlife.

Heartworm

The heartworm, *Dirofilaria immitis*, is a serious parasite. It lives in the bloodstream, eventually blocking the heart chambers and the blood supply to the lungs. In heavy infestations, the animal can collapse and die. It is transmitted by mosquitoes sucking blood (and, therefore, worms) from the animal, and then moving on to another dog for another snack. The mosquitoes live only in warm climates, so some countries, such as the U.K., are not affected by this dangerous parasite. Selamectin, mentioned previously, is one of the effective drugs available. Consult your veterinarian if heartworm is a problem in your area.

Yorkies living in warm climates must be treated for heartworm.

Other intestinal worms

Hookworms (*uncinaria* and *ancylostoma* species), together with whipworms (*Trichuris vulpis*), are occasionally the cause of lack of condition. More severe signs, such as anemia or dysentery, can occur. In the U.K., these worms are usually associated with kenneled dogs. They are often discovered during routine fecal investigation rather than because the dog is sick.

Treatment is uncomplicated with modern preparations from your veterinarian.

Protozoan parasites

Giardia and coccidia are gut parasites that can cause diarrhea, particularly in puppies. Giardia is a water-borne disease, more common in North America than in Britain. The disease can occur in the U.K. in imported dogs, and is likely to increase with the relaxation of quarantine regulations.

Giardiasis is considered to be zoonotic and is the most common intestinal parasite in humans in America. Nevertheless, there is no conclusive evidence that cysts shed by dogs (and cats) are infective to humans.

Certain blood-borne protozoan parasites, such as babesia and leishmania, are important in southern parts of America and Europe, but, at present, do not regularly occur in Britain. Leishmania, spread by sandflies, constitutes a public health risk.

FIRST AID

Because of their inherent active nature, Yorkshire Terriers can get themselves into all sorts of scrapes. A basic knowledge of canine first aid, therefore, never is amiss.

First aid is the initial treatment given in any emergency. The purpose is to preserve life, reduce pain and discomfort, minimize the risk of permanent disability or disfigurement, and to prevent further injury.

Emergency procedures

In an emergency, you will find it easier to follow a standard procedure:

1. Do not panic.
2. Make sure you are safe.
3. Get help if possible.
4. Assess the situation.
5. Contact your veterinarian as soon as possible.
6. Try to keep the patient still. A cardboard box or other makeshift container is perfect for a

Yorkie. Use the box to convey the dog to the veterinarian as soon as possible, but make sure that he cannot jump out.
7. Drive carefully and observe the speed limits.

Assessment

A is for Airway. Is the dog breathing? Is there any obstruction in the airway?
B is for Bleeding. Is there any hemorrhage?
C is for Consciousness. Has he collapsed or is he convulsing?

Imagine a dog choking because there is something lodged in the mouth or throat:
A. Try to remove any obstruction. Take care! If conscious, even the most gentle pet is likely to bite in fear. Use a stick, or some other blunt implement, to gently dislodge anything in the mouth. Wrap something round the stick to clear vomit or saliva from the airway.
B. Check the color of the mucous membranes of the gums, or inside the lips. If the dog is bleeding and shocked, these membranes will be pale or white. If bleeding is visible (i.e., external), try to stop it, otherwise treat for shock. Check for heartbeat and respiration by placing your hand around the chest, just behind the forelegs, and try to detect movement. If not, start cardiopulmonary resuscitation (CPR).

CPR is not difficult in a Yorkie. The heart is situated in the lower part of the chest, about level with the elbows. Place your hand around the sternum (chest), your fingers one side and your thumb the other. Start gently squeezing approximately 20-25 times a minute. This has the dual function of stimulating the heart and helps to get air into the lungs. About every 10 squeezes, check for a heartbeat and breathing. If you are successful, continue for several minutes. Once the heart is beating, a vague, pink tinge should return to the mucous membranes.

C. If the dog has collapsed but is breathing, try to get him to the veterinarian as soon as possible. Otherwise, continue CPR for at least 10 minutes on site. If convulsing, proceed as below.

Shock

Shock is a complex condition disrupting the delicate fluid balance of the body. It is always accompanied by a serious fall in blood pressure. Causes include serious hemorrhage, heart failure, heatstroke, and acute allergic reactions, e.g., beestings.

Signs of shock include:
1. Rapid breathing
2. Rapid heart rate
3. Pale mucous membranes
4. Severe depression
5. A cold feel to the limbs, ears, etc.
6. Sometimes vomiting.

The most important first aid treatment for shock is to maintain body heat. Avoid external heat; instead wrap the dog in a blanket or towel and get him to your veterinarian quickly.

The responsible owner should learn the principles of first aid.

First aid procedures

Here are a few examples of basic first aid procedures:

Bleeding: Torn nails are fairly common in Yorkshire Terriers, and can result in copious bleeding. Any hemorrhage from the limbs should be bandaged fairly tightly using any clean material.

Bleeding from other parts of the body (e.g., head, ears, etc.) that cannot be bandaged easily, should be controlled by applying a cold-water swab, and finger or hand pressure. Seek veterinary help.

Burns and scalds: Cool the burned or scalded area with cold water. If the injury is due to a caustic substance (e.g., drain cleaner or bleach), wash with plenty of cold water, and get professional advice without delay. This will often avoid the burned/scalded area sloughing skin a few days later.

Eye injuries: Due to the Yorkshire Terrier's exuberant lifestyle, scratches from bushes and cats' claws are common injuries. Cold water, or, better still, saline solution (contact lens solution), liberally applied with a pad, should be used to cleanse the eye. If the eyeball appears to be injured, or if there is any bleeding, try to cover with a pad soaked in cold water, and get to your veterinarian as soon as possible.

Heatstroke: In warm, humid weather, heatstroke can strike rapidly. Sunrooms and poorly ventilated rooms can be just as dangerous as cars. Heatstroke can occur without the dog being in direct sunlight.

First signs are excessive panting with obvious breathing distress (stertor). Coma and death can quickly follow due to irreversible changes in the blood vessels. Reduce the temperature as quickly as possible. Plunge or bathe the dog in cold water. Place ice on the gums, under the tail, and in the groin. Then take the wet animal to the veterinarian as soon as possible.

Fits and seizures: During a fit (seizure), the dog is unconscious and oblivious to what is happening. Nevertheless, it is pretty terrifying for onlookers. To prevent injury during the fit (and afterwards, until he is fully conscious), confinement in a cardboard box is useful.

Subdued light hastens recovery. Most seizures last only a very short time, but it will seem an age to you. If the dog is seizuring for more than five minutes, call your veterinarian for advice. Otherwise, take him in, once conscious, for a checkup.

BREED-PRONE PROBLEMS

Compared with other members of the Toy Group, Yorkshire Terriers have few genuine breed-prone problems. Those that do occur are not unique, but are shared with other small dogs.

Common problems include dental problems, joint problems, plus coughing and breathing problems as a result of tracheal collapse.

Dental problems

Yorkshire Terriers, together with many other tiny dogs, are well known for their dental problems. These often start when a pup is just a few months old before the permanent teeth are fully erupted. Sometimes, the baby teeth are not shed, and, often, the puppy will appear to have a double set of teeth (double dentition). It is then essential that the temporary teeth are extracted so that the permanent teeth are not displaced, causing malocclusion. Examine your puppy's teeth regularly as part of the grooming routine, and consult your veterinarian if you have any worries.

Once the permanent teeth have erupted, it is important to preserve them! Periodontitis (inflammation of the structures surrounding the tooth) is very common in the breed. Once established, periodontitis soon leads to loss of teeth, which is the reason why so many "gummy" Yorkshire Terriers are seen at a relatively young age.

Dental home care, which includes regular brushing and special dental treats, will delay – if not prevent – the condition. It is essential to start dental care early, so mention it to the veterinarian when you take your puppy in for primary vaccinations.

Tracheal collapse

The windpipe or trachea is a tube from the larynx to the lungs. The lumen is kept open by a series of cartilaginous rings. In the Yorkshire Terrier and other Toy breeds, these sometimes fail, resulting in a chronic cough, which is often induced by excitement. Signs can start when the puppy is only a few months old, when it is noticed that pulling on the lead is followed by a typical "goose honking" cough.

Treatment depends on the severity of the condition, and the amount of flattening or other deformity of the tracheal rings. In some cases, special surgery is required. However, many cases, particularly those of adult onset, can be managed medically. If you are at all concerned about your Yorkie's breathing, seek advice at an early stage.

Orthopedic problems

1. Legg-Calve Perthes disease
More descriptively called aseptic or avascular necrosis of the femoral head, this is a crippling disease of small, immature dogs, particularly

Despite his dainty size, the Yorkie suffers few breed-specific problems.

terriers. It is seen frequently in Yorkshire Terriers, usually at about five months of age. The puppy is noticed to be lame on one or both hind legs. Increasing pain and restriction of movement are noted.

In many breeds, the condition is known to be hereditary. Affected individuals should not be bred from. Due to reduction to the blood supply to the growing femoral head, which is the "ball" of the "ball and socket" hip joint, part of the bone dies and the joint becomes progressively distorted. This results in pain, and, ultimately, total loss of use of the leg. Treatment, which involves removal of the diseased bone, is usually very successful.

With good care and management, your Yorkie should live a long and healthy life.   *Misha by Varva Photography.*

2. Luxating patellae

Slipping kneecaps (luxating patellae) are basically joint problems. The patella (kneecap) moves in a groove at the lower end of the femur (thighbone). Some dogs are born with a groove that is not deep enough to retain the kneecap, so that it "pops out" of the groove, usually to the inside of the joint (medial patella luxation). This causes the dog to hop for a few steps. In mild cases, the kneecap often returns to its groove, and lamenesss disappears.

Both legs can be affected, and if your Yorkie is overweight, the condition can be crippling. Often the condition first becomes noticeable when the pup is only a few months old. Intermittently, he appears to hop on one of the hind legs. These are the same signs as seen initially with Perthes disease, described above.

Today, there are very successful surgical techniques available to correct the problem, particularly if it is diagnosed early, before arthritic changes start. Consult your veterinarian if you are worried about the hind leg movement of your growing Yorkshire Terrier. It may not be that "he has overdone it and is just a bit stiff." It is wise to refrain from breeding from any affected individuals.

SIGNING OFF

We are lucky that the Yorkshire Terrier is generally a fit, active dog, and with good care and management, your Yorkie should suffer few major health problems. Take your responsibilities as an owner seriously, working on preventive health care, giving the correct diet and exercise, caring for the coat, and ensuring that your dog has plenty of mental stimulation. If you follow these guidelines, you will be rewarded with many years of happy companionship with a dog that will give you love, loyalty, and entertainment in abundance.